ADVANCES IN PUBLIC HEALTH AND NUTRITION SERIES

MID DAY MEAL PROGRAMME

PAST, PRESENT AND FUTURE

ADVANCES IN PUBLIC HEALTH AND NUTRITION SERIES

MID DAY MEAL PROGRAMME
PAST, PRESENT AND FUTURE

By

Dr. **Vanisha S. Nambiar**

(M.Sc, Ph.D., Nutrition)
Associate Professor
Department of Foods & Nutrition
The Maharaja SayajiRao University of Baroda
Gujarat (India)

&

Ms. **Rujuta K. Desai**

(M.Sc, Public Health Nutrition)
Department of Foods & Nutrition
Faculty of Family & Community Science
The M.S. University of Baroda
Gujarat (India)

DISCOVERY PUBLISHING HOUSE PVT. LTD.
NEW DELHI-110 002

Published by:
Tilak Wasan
DISCOVERY PUBLISHING HOUSE PVT. LTD.
4383/4B, Ansari Road, Darya Ganj
New Delhi-110 002 (India)
Phone : +91-11-23279245, 43596064-65
Fax : +91-11-23253475
E-mail : discoverypublishinghouse@gmail.com
sales@discoverypublishinggroup.com
parul.wasan@gmail.com
web : www.discoverypublishinggroup.com

First Edition: **2014**

ISBN: 978-93-5056-441-7

Mid Day Meal Programme
Past, Present and Future

Printed at:
Dynamic Printers
Delhi

Preface

Even after 64 years of Independence, India has the dubious distinction of having one of the highest prevalence (over 50%) of under nutrition (stunting, wasting, and micronutrient deficiencies like anemia, vitamin A deficiency and others), in the world. Such high prevalence of under nutrition among school going children, not only undermines educational attainments and productivity, but also has adverse implications for income and economic growth of the nation.

This book, **Mid Day Meal Programme:** ***Past, Present and Future,*** is 1st in the series of Advances in Public Health Nutrition. The book discusses various developmental programmes which are initiatives of the Government of India including the National programme of Nutritional support to primary education (NP-NSPE) commonly known as the Mid Day Meal Programme (MDMP).

India's Mid day meal scheme is the world's largest school feeding programme and is considered as a means of promoting improved enrolment, school attendance and retention. Simultaneously, it may improve the nutritional status of primary school children. With children from all castes and communities eating together, it is also a means of bringing about better social integration. The National Programme of Nutritional Support to Primary Education (NP-NSPE) was launched as a Centrally Sponsored Scheme on 15th August 1995, initially in 2408 blocks in the country. By the year 1997-98 the NP-NSPE was introduced in all blocks of the country. It was further extended in 2002 to cover not only children in classes I-V of government, government aided and local body schools, but also children studying in centers run under the Education Guarantee Scheme (EGS) and Alternative and innovative Education Scheme (AIE). The Mid day meal scheme also aims to provide nutritional support to children of primary stage in drought-affected areas during summer vacation.

The book highlights the journey of the MDMP and focuses on the innumerous advantages of the same if implemented in line with the NP-NSPE norms. Drawbacks such as poor logistics, inadequate political support, unawareness and lack of training to grass root level functionaries are also reflected in the book which is the culmination of reviews of assorted studies of the MDMP reported across the country.

The book also includes the detailed methodology and results of a research project which focused on Monitoring and evaluation of the Mid Day Meal Scheme in 10 schools of Rural Vadodara. It includes details about the enrolment, attendance, category rate and gender in the MDM covered schools; actual facts about the Mid Day Meal kitchen infrastructure and management, School Infrastructure and management; Nutritive value, Quality and Quantity of the meal served under MDM. It also covers the qualitative methodology and results of the Knowledge, Attitude and Practices of the Teachers, Students and MDM Staff regarding Mid Day Meal Scheme.

The book addresses these critical issues and highlights the past, present and future of this massive programme. This book will be useful for developmental workers, policy makers and government and non government organizations involved with the education or community development work. It will be an asset for the academicians' involved in public health and nutrition. This book will be helpful to the graduate and post graduate students of public health and nutrition, social work and preventive and community medicine.

Dr. Vanisha S. Nambiar

Ms Rujuta K. Desai

Contents

Glossary

1.	Global Hunger Index	GHI
2.	International Food Policy Research Institute	IFPRI
3.	India State Hunger Index	ISHI
4.	Millennium Development Goals	MDG
5.	Integrated Child Development Services	ICDS
6.	Oral Rehydration Therapy	ORT
7.	Acute Respiratory Infections	ARI
8.	Jananisurakshayojana	JSY
9.	Prevention Maternal Mortality Programme	PMM
10.	Intermittent Preventive Treatment	IPT
11.	Nutrition Programme for Adolescent Girls	NPAG
12.	Sarva Shiksha Abhiyan	SSA
13.	National Nutrition Mission	NNM
14.	Mid Day Meal Programme	MDMP
15.	Convention on the Rights of the Child	CRC
16.	Health Systems Research	HSR
17.	Rapid Appraisal Survey	RAS
18.	Behaviour Change Approaches	BCC
19.	Catholic Relief Service	CRS
20.	Church World Service	CWS
21.	Expanded Nutrition Programme	ENP
22.	Applied Nutrition Programme	ANP

Development of India

Improvement in the quality of life is the central pillar of India's planned development. The adult literacy rate improved from 18.3 per cent in 1951 to 65.4 per cent in 2001. India now has the world's largest trained workforce in science, administration and technology. Attempts are under way to ensure universal primary education and to improve secondary and vocational education. Efforts are also being made to ensure that higher and technical education gets due attention (Ramachandran, 2005).

Although urban amenities have failed to cope with the increase in population, cities and towns have become the engines of social change, rapid economic development and improved access to education, employment and health care. Rural and urban populations continue to lack access to safe drinking-water (38% in 1981 and 68% in 2001) and good environmental sanitation (less than 30%). With better communication and transportation, urban and rural areas can be linked, both economically and socially, to create an urban-rural continuum of communities and to achieve sustained, rapid improvement in quality of life in both (Ramachandran, 2005).

After over 60 years of independence, India has the dubious distinction of having one of the highest prevalence (over 50%) of under nutrition (stunting, wasting, and micronutrient deficiencies like anaemia, vitamin A deficiency and others), in the world. Efforts made since independence have made only marginal impact. Malnutrition is seriously and adversely impacting the country's development, and health care expenditure (INSA, 2009).

GLOBAL HUNGER INDEX AND INDIA

The Global Hunger Index (GHI) is a tool adapted and developed with a multidimensional approach by International Food Policy Research Institute (IFPRI) for regularly describing the state of global hunger. The GHI incorporates three equally weighted indicators:

1. The proportion of undernourished as a percentage of the population (reflecting the share of the population with insufficient dietary energy intake).
2. The prevalence of underweight in children under the age of five (indicating the proportion of children suffering from weight loss).
3. The mortality rate of children under the age of five (partially reflecting the fatal synergy between inadequate dietary intake and unhealthy environments).

The index ranks countries on a 100-point scale, with 0 being the best score (no hunger) and 100 being the worst, though neither of these extremes is achieved in practice. Values less than 4.9 reflect low hunger, values between five and 9.9 reflect moderate hunger, values between ten and 19.9 indicate a serious problem, values between 20 and 29.9 are alarming, and values of 30 or higher are extremely alarming (IFPRI, 2008).

India is ranked a poor 65th in battling hunger, according to the Global Hunger Index for 2009. It said 21 per cent of the Indian population was undernourished (between 2003 and 2005), 43.5 per cent Indian children under the age of five were underweight (between 2002 and 2007) and the under five-year age infant mortality rate in 2007 was 7.2 per cent (Global Hunger Index Report, 2008).

EDUCATION AMONG SCHOOL CHILDREN IN INDIA

Over six decades of independence, half of India's children are illiterate, thus "Identification of Primary Education" as a key thrust area seems a mere lip service of education policy. Nearly 52 per cent of girls aged 6-10 and 48 per cent of boys aged 6-10 are out of school (Kumar, 2011).

According to the Indian Constitution, elementary education is a fundamental right of children in the age group of 6-14 years. India has about 688,000 primary schools and 110,000 secondary schools (Kumar, 2011). In a financially and socially developed state like Gujarat, only 71 per cent of children aged 6-17 years attend school, with somewhat higher prevalence in the urban areas (74%) than in rural areas (69%). Ninety per cent of primary-school age children (6-10 years) attend school (92% in urban areas and 89% in rural areas), while it drops to 74 per cent for 11-14 years children and further falls to 32 per cent for 15-17 years children. Thus the difference in the urban and rural school attendance rates increases with children's age (NFHS 3, 2005-06).

At least half of all students from rural area drop out before completing school. Several persisting problems persist such as 'social' distance – arising out of caste, class and gender differences – denies children equal opportunities in attaining education. Child labour in some parts of the country and resistance to sending girls to school remains a constant concern (UNICEF, 2010).

On the other hand the education system faces a shortage of resources; schools, classrooms and teachers. There are also concerns relating to teacher training, the quality of the curriculum, assessment of learning achievements and the efficacy of school management. Given the scarcity of quality schools, many children drop out before completing five years of primary education (UNICEF, 2010).

FOOD SECURITY AMONG SCHOOL CHILDREN IN INDIA

School age is a sensitive period in children's development.Children need to consume sufficient food of the right quality in order to thrive. Hunger can curtail on their fundamental capacity of learning and can prevent them from making the most of their abilities and opportunities.

According to the report of "The World Bank" (2009), India ranks 2nd in the world of the number of malnourished children, where 47% of the children exhibit a degree of malnutrition. The prevalence of underweight children in India is amongst the highest in the world.

The nutritional status scenario of school going children in the urban and rural India is changing. Underweight prevalence is higher in rural areas (50%) than in urban areas (38%); higher among girls (48.9%) than among boys (45.5%); higher among scheduled castes (53.2%) and scheduled tribes (56.2%) than among other castes (44.1%); and although underweight is pervasive throughout the wealth distribution, the prevalence of underweight reaches as high as 60 per cent in the lowest wealth quintile (Gragnolati et al, 2005).

Social and public health scientists have undertaken immense work in the area and have established facts and figures of the nutritional status of the children across the country. School age children in states such as Rajasthan, Gujarat, Delhi, Maharashtra and West Bengal have shown predominance existence of clinical signs and symptoms of IDA, VAD and IDD at various degrees, with meagre difference between the genders. Though 3/4th of school going children consume more than 70 per cent of RDA for energy, the intakes of micronutrients such as iron, iodine and vitamin A are inadequate (Vyas and Choudhry (2005), Kapil and Sethi (2004), Mukhopadhyay et al (2005).

In specific to Gujarat, 44.7 per cent of children are underweight and 22.3 per cent of the population is undernourished. Such a health condition is also coupled with abnormal haematological indices and cell morphologies which when supplemented with green gram whole, bengal gram whole, drumsticks and lemon juice have shown reduction in the symptoms of micronutrient deficiencies by 28.57 per cent;

thus emphasising on the interdependence of nutrients and importance of nutritional security (Nambiar and Parnami, 2005).

Above all, India is also facing the challenge of dual burden of malnutrition with simultaneous increase in the number of over nourished and under nourished children, vulnerable during their period of growth spurt. This call for redefining "Food Security" as "Availability of Right Quality and Adequate Amount" of food complemented with the education of the same. One of the prerequisites to fight poverty in the long term lies in education. Education is one of the most effective ways to improve food security andstrengthen coping strategies for times of crisis. Thus providing Food for Education helps break the poverty cycle and encouraging education gives hope to the future generations.

National Schemes and Programmes
Strides by Indian Government

The Millennium Development Goals (MDG's) encapsulate the development aspirations of the world as a whole. MDG's are used as a bench mark for measuring the success of any programme by assessing its outcome indicators (MDG, 2008). Advancement towards the MDG's depends on government institutions, services and support, such as schools, health facilities, agricultural extension and physical infrastructure, as well as trade and interchange with others.

Government of India has taken several initiatives to attain the MDG's. Among the numerous programmes undertaken by the government; some of the most important ones are as listed below:

Schemes to eradicate poverty and hunger:

1. Sampoorna Grameen RozgarYojana (Total Rural Employment Scheme)
2. The Swarnajayanti Gram Swarojgar Yojana (Golden Jubilee Rural Self-Employment Scheme)
3. The Indira AwaasYojana (Indira Housing Scheme)
4. National Slum Development Programme
5. The Swarna Jayanti Shahari RozgarYojana (Golden Jubilee Urban Employment Scheme)
6. The Valmiki Ambedkar Awaas Yojana (Housing Scheme)
7. Mid day meal programme

Schemes to achieve universal primary education:

1. Sarva Shiksha Abhiyan
2. District Primary Education Programme
3. National Programme Of Nutritional Support to Primary Education (MDMP)
4. Primary Education Enhancement Project

(MDG Report, 2005)

Schemes to promote gender equality and empower women:

1. Adolescent Girl Scheme
2. Kishori Shakti Yojana
3. Balika SamridhiYojana
4. National Policy for the Empowerment of Women

(MHFW, 2007)

Schemes to reduce child mortality:

1. National Rural Health Mission
2. The Oral Rehydration Therapy (ORT) Programme
3. Acute Respiratory Infections (ARI) Control Programme
4. Integrated Child Development Services

(NRHM, 2007)

Schemes to improve maternal health:

1. Integrated Child Development Services (ICDS)
2. Integrated intervention programme- NRHM & RCH II
3. Janani Suraksha Yojana (JSY)
4. Safe-Motherhood Initiative
5. Prevention Maternal Mortality Programme (PMM)
6. Making Pregnancy Safer Initiative
7. Maternal and Neonatal Health Programme Maternal Health Project
8. Prevention and Management of Safe Abortion Programme
9. Intermittent Preventive Treatment (IPT)

(NRHM, 2007)

Schemes to combat HIV/AIDS, malaria and other disease:

1. National AIDS Control Organisation
2. National AIDS Control Programme III
3. Project Ahavan
4. National Tuberculosis Control Programme
5. National Malaria Control Project
6. National Vector Borne Disease Control Programme

Schemes to ensure environmental sustainability:

1. Rural Water Supply Programme
2. Swajaldhara
3. Central Rural Sanitation Programme
4. Sulabh Shauchalaya
5. Van Mahotsav

Schemes to develop global partnership:

1. Accelerated child survival and development programme.
2. Bill & melinda gates
3. Adolescence education programmes
5. Education for all international coordination

Specific schemes for health, nutritional and educational benefits of children:

1. **Child line Service:** Launched during year 1998-99. It provides emergency assistance to a child. The child is referred to an appropriate organisation for long-term follow up and care.
2. **An Integrated Programme for Street Children:** Works to prevent destitution of children and facilitate their withdrawal from life on the streets. The programme provides for shelter, nutrition, health care, education, recreation facilities to street children, and seeks to protect them against abuse and exploitation by developing awareness and provide support to build capacity of the Government, NGOs and the community at large to realize

the rights of the child enshrined in the UN Convention on the Rights of the Child (CRC) and in the Juvenile Justice (Care and Protection of Children) Act, 2000.

3. **Welfare of working children in need of care and protection:** The programme provides opportunities such as non-formal education, vocational training, etc, to working children to facilitate their entry/re-entry into mainstream education in cases where they have either not attended any learning system or where for some reasons their education has been discontinued with a view to preventing their continued or future exploitation.
4. **Nutrition Programme for Adolescent Girls (NPAG):** The programme aims to address the problem of under-nutrition among adolescent girls, pregnant women and lactating mothers, since year 2002-03. The government provides 6 kg of free food-grains to undernourished adolescent girls; for which funds are given as 100% grant to States/UTs so that they can provide food grains through the Public Distribution System free of cost to the families of identified undernourished individuals.
5. **Kishori Shakti Yojana:** The broad objectives of the Scheme are to improve the nutritional, health and development status of adolescent girls, promote awareness of health, hygiene, nutrition and family care, link them to opportunities for learning life skills, going back to school. It seeks to empower adolescent girls, so as to enable them to take charge of their livesand is viewed as a holistic initiative for the development of adolescent girls.
6. **Balika Samridhi Yojana**: Major objectives of the programme are to change negative family and community attitudes towards the girl child at birth and towards her mother, to improve enrolment and retention of girl children in schools, to raise the age at marriage of girls and to assist the girl to undertake income generating activities.

7. **National Nutrition Policy:** It was adopted by the Government of India in 1993 under the aegis of the department of women and child development.The policy advocates the monitoring the nutrition levels across the country and sensitising government machinery on the need for good nutrition and prevention of malnutrition. The Food and Nutrition Board, included within develops posters, audio jingles and video spots for disseminating correct facts about breastfeeding and complementary feeding.
8. **National charter for action:** It emphasizes Government of India's commitment to children's rights to survival, health and nutrition, standard of living, play and leisure, early childhood care, education, protection of the girl child, empowering adolescents, equality, life and liberty, name and nationality, freedom of expression, freedom of association and peaceful assembly, the right to a family and the right to be protected from economic exploitation and all forms of abuse.
9. **Integrated Child Development Scheme (ICDS):** Launched on 2nd October 1975 in 33 Community Development Blocks; today represents one of the world's largest programmes for early childhood development. It is the foremost symbol of India's commitment to her children – India's response to the challenge of providing pre-school education on one hand and breaking the vicious cycle of malnutrition, morbidity, reduced learning capacity and mortality, on the other. It is an inter-sectoral programme which seeks to directly reach out to children, below six years, especially from vulnerable and remote areas and give them a head-start by providing an integrated programme of early childhood education, health and nutrition (ICDS).
10. **Sarva Shiksha Abhiyan (SSA):** Sarva Shiksha Abhiyan (SSA) is Government of India's flagship programme for achievement of Universalization of Elementary Education (UEE) in a time bound manner, as mandated by 86th

amendment to the Constitution of India making free and compulsory Education to the Children of 6-14 years age group, a Fundamental Right.

The programme seeks to open new schools in those habitations which do not have schooling facilities and strengthen existing school infrastructure through provision of additional class rooms, toilets, drinking water, maintenance grant and school improvement grants. Existing schools with inadequate teacher strength are provided with additional teachers, while the capacity of existing teachers is being strengthened by extensive training, grants for developing teaching-learning materials and strengthening of the academic support structure at a cluster, block and district level (SSA).

11. **National Nutrition Mission (NNM):** The basic objective of the Mission will be to address the problem of malnutrition in a holistic manner and accelerate reduction in various forms of malnutrition specially in women and children such as under nutrition, anemia, vitamin A deficiency, iodine deficiency disorders and chronic energy deficiency in adults so as to reduce prevalence of low birth weight, infant mortality rate, child mortality rate and maternal mortality rate.

(MWCD, 2011)

MID DAY MEAL PROGRAMME

The world's largest school feeding programme, The Mid Day Meal programme, aims to cover all students from classes I-V in Government, Government aided schools. The Programme has the key objectives of: protecting children from classroom hunger, increasing school enrolment and attendance, improved socialization among children belonging to all castes, addressing malnutrition, and social empowerment through provision of employment to women.

The major objectives of the mid day meal scheme are:

1. Improving the nutritional status of children in classes I-VIII in Government, Local Body and Government aided schools, and EGS and AIE centres.

2. Encouraging poor children, belonging to disadvantaged sections, to attend school more regularly and help them concentrate on classroom activities.
3. Providing nutritional support to children of primary stage in drought-affected areas during summer vacation.

Mid Day Meal in schools has had a long history in India. In 1925, a Mid Day Meal Programme was introduced for disadvantaged children in Madras Municipal Corporation. By the mid 1980s three States viz. Gujarat, Kerala and Tamil Nadu and the UT of Pondicherry had universalized a cooked Mid Day Meal Programme with their own resources for children studying at the primary stage. Mid Day Meal was also being provided to children in Tribal Areas in some States like Madhya Pradesh and Orissa. By 1990-91 the number of States implementing the mid day meal programme with their own resources on a universal or a large scale had increased to twelve, namely, Goa, Gujarat, Kerala, Madhya Pradesh, Maharashtra, Meghalaya, Mizoram, Nagaland, Sikkim, Tamil Nadu, Tripura and Uttar Pradesh. In another three States, namely Karnataka, Orissa and West Bengal, the programme was being implemented with State resources in combination with international assistance. Another two States, namely Andhra Pradesh and Rajasthan were implementing the programme entirely with international assistance (NPNSPE, 2006).

NEED FOR THE OVERVIEW OF THE SCHEMES AND PROGRAMMES

The brief look at various programmes and their objectives undertaken by the government of India emphasises the commitment of the government and its investments in the future of its children and nation as a whole.

As per 2001 census, India has around 157.86 million children, constituting 15.42 per cent of India's population, who are below the age of 6 years. Of these 75.95 million children are girls and remaining 81.91 million children are boys. The sex ratio among children (0-6 years) as per Census 2001 is 927 i.e. 927 females per 1000 males.

Table 2.1

Annual Budget for Some National Programmes/Ministries

(Rs. In crores)

Programmes/Ministries	Target Group	Budget 2010-11
Ministry of Women and Child Development • Integrated Child Development Scheme (ICDS) • National Programme for Adolescent Girls (NPAG)	Women of reproductive age and 0-5yr. of childrenAdolescent girls	29158.13
Ministry of Health and Family Welfare • Reproductive & Child Health Project (RCH II)	Women of reproductive age and children (0-6 months)	10841.48
Department of School Education • Sarva Shiksha Abhiyaan (SSA) • Mid-day Meal (MDM) District Primary Education	6-14 year Children	28079.30

Ministry of Finance, 2010-11

A significant proportion of these children live in economic and social environment which impedes the child's physical and mental development. These conditions include poverty, poor environmental sanitation, disease, infection, inadequate access to primary health care, inappropriate child caring and feeding practices etc (MWCD, 2007).

Moreover, as per the 2011 census, the growth rate of population for India in the last decade was 17.64 with 12.18 per cent in rural and 31.80 per cent in theurban areas. Bihar (23.90%) exhibited the highest decadal growth rate in rural population. India's population in 1901 was about 238.4 million, which has increased by more than four times in 110 years to reach a population of 1,210 million in 2011.

Thus there is a rapid increase in the burden and challenges for the government to meet the balance and fill the lapse, for satisfactory attainment of the MDG's. In order to achieve the set objectives, every year the government is expending huge amount behind various programmes. A glance at the budgets sanctioned for few of the ministries.

Beginning of "Food for Education" in India

MID DAY MEAL SCHEME: REMINISCENCE

The concept of Mid-Day Meal has a long history in India. In 1925, a Midday Meal Programme was introduced for children belonging to poor socioeconomic status in Madras Corporation area.

In 1928, Keshav Academy of Calcutta introduced compulsory Mid-Day Tiffin for school boys on payment basis at the rate of four annas per child per month. In 1941, in parts of Kerala, the School Lunch Programme was started, while in 1942, Bombay started implementing a free Mid-Day Meal Scheme.

A Mid-Day Meal Scheme was introduced in Bangalore city in 1946, to provide cooked rice and yoghurt. In 1953, Uttar Pradesh Government introduced a scheme, on voluntary basis, to provide meals consisting of boiled or roasted or sprouted grams, ground-nut, puffed rice, boiled potatoes or seasonal fruits.

In the 1950s, many States came to introduce mid-day meal programmes with the assistance of different international agencies like UNICEF, FAO and WHO. International voluntary/charity organisations like Catholic Relief Service (CRS), Church World Service (CWS), and CARE, USA's Meals for Million, etc, also came forward to assist in these programmes. During 1958-59, an Expanded Nutrition Programme (ENP) was introduced jointly by FAO, WHO,

UNICEF and Government of India was introduced, and subsequently expanded into Applied Nutrition Programme (ANP).

It was also suggested that a Participatory monitoring effort on the food for work Programme on a pilot basis should be taken up in a few districts to study the outcome by identifying proper indicators and involving civil society participatory networks that exist at the grassroots level. The broad features of the programme were:

- Coverage of primary school children in a phased manner to cover 9.54 crore children by the end of the seventh Plan; the estimated expenditure for the whole plan being Rs.4000 crore.
- Provision of uniform nutrition for the children at 300 calories per day with 12-15 grams of protein (100 grams of cereal, 10 grams of dal and 5 grams of edible oil).
- Expenditure per child, including expenses on administration to be 60 paise.
- FCI to release food grains at Central Issue Prices; the value of which to be counted against Central assistance to State, estimated Central assistance for the year 1989-90 being reckoned at Rs. 623.50 crore State shall make arrangements for pulse and oil.
- Linkage of implementation of the scheme with existing civil supplies distribution system.
- Supply of rations to be in kind and deliveries thereof be made through State/cooperative agencies.
- Central assistance to be limited to 50 per cent.
- Each State to have its own specific scheme with appropriate infrastructure and delivery systems subject to laid down parameters.
- Funds to be provided, for the programme not to be construed as part of the outlay under the Head 'Education'.
- Funds required for the programme to come from provisions earmarked for poverty alleviation scheme.

- States should evolve suitable logistics and make arrangements for cooks, helpers, administration, supervision and monitoring.
- Community involvement in the implementation of the scheme.

It was recognized that the scheme had certain inherent problems such as possibilities of leakage, inadequacy of buildings, non- attendance of teachers, participation by non-school going children, abuse by those incharge, etc.

The Fifth All India Educational Survey had brought out the following facts on the coverage of mid-day meals in 1986. Free mid-day meals were provided to 15.91 per cent primary school students and to 25.93 per cent upper primary school students. Inter-state variations ranged from nil coverage in Manipur to 46.14 per cent in Sikkim, 47.55 per cent in Tamil Nadu, 47.84 per cent in West Bengal, 53.23 per cent in Dadra and Nagar Haveli, 56.07 per cent in Tripura and 59.94 per cent in Lakshadweep at the primary level. In rural areas, 28.28 per cent primary, 25.06 per cent upper primary, 7.51 per cent secondary and 11.8 per cent higher secondary schools had provision for mid-day meals as against 24.75 per cent primary, 20.91 per cent upper primary, 6.31 per cent secondary and 11.84 per cent higher secondary schools in urban areas.

There were 22.6 million students who were availing of this facility at all levels of school education; of these 78.41 per cent were studying in rural schools, 40.98 per cent were girls, 20.05 per cent were Scheduled Caste Children and 12.81 per cent were Scheduled Tribe children (PO&RM, 2005).

On August 15, 1995 National Programme of Nutritional Support to Primary Education was launched as a Centrally Sponsored Scheme to boost Universalisation of Primary Education by increasing enrollment, retention and attendance and simultaneously impacting on nutrition of the students in primary classes.

Even six years after its introduction, most of the states preferred dry rations to cooked meals, to the children (NAC,

2004). Therefore the Supreme Court intervened with its directions specifying the implementation norms for MDM. Thus the programme was implemented with following objectives:

- Improving the nutritional status of children in classes I-V in Government, Local Body and Government aided schools, and EGS and AIE centres.
- Encouraging poor children, belonging to disadvantaged sections, to attend school more regularly and help them concentrate on classroom activities.
- Providing nutritional support to children of primary stage in drought-affected areas during summer vacation.

The NP-NSPE has provided with guidelines on implementation, organisation and management of the mid-day meal programme.

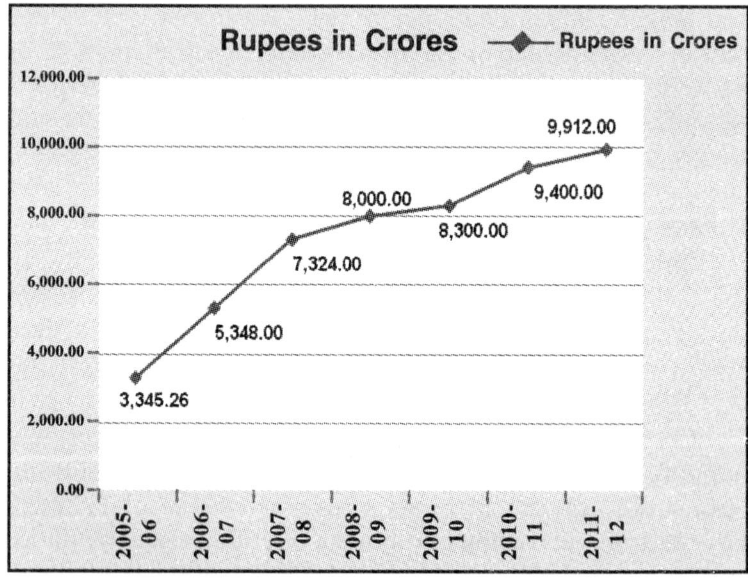

Fig. 3.1: Comparison of the Yearly Budget Allocation at the Central Level for MDM

Ministry of Finance, 2011-2012

Table 3.1

Parameters Stated Under the NP-NSPE Guidelines

Parameters	Guidelines	Guidelines 2010-11
1	2	3
Central assistance	• Free food grains (wheat/rice) @100 grams per child per School Day from the nearest FCI go down.	• 175 gm ration for primary and 262 gm ration for upper primary including vegetables and oil.
	• Cooking cost @ Re 1 per child per school day	• Cost per child inclusive of all 2.02 for primary and 3.02 for upper primary. This would be revised by 7.5 per cent every year in April.
	• Reimburse the actual cost incurred in transportation of food grains of Rs.75 per quintal.	
	• Management, monitoring and evaluation costs @ 2 per cent of the cost of food grains, transport subsidy and cooking assistance.	

(Contd…)

1	2	3
Expenditure by State	• Contributes a minimum of 50 paise, and bears the cost of providing meal to students of standard VI-VII	• Cost per child 1.67 for primary and 1.15 for upper primary children
Menu/ Recepies	• 50 gm rice, 50 gm wheat, 20 gm dal, 10 gm oil and 50 gm vegetables per child which = 180 gm of ration/day/child which should be equivalent to 450 Kcal, 12 gm proteins and be adequate in micro nutrients.	• 650 Kcal and 12 gm proteins for primary and 900 Kcal and 20 gm proteins for upper primary classes to be provided in a day.
	• Incorporation of seasonal and available vegetables should be done.	• Fruits 2/week
	• Menu should provide variety and must be flexible for local taste and culture acceptance.	
Sanitation and hygiene	• Training the MDM staff on personal hygiene and safe food handling	• Training the MDM staff on personal hygiene and safe food handling.
	• Cooking and serving area should be clean	• Cooking and serving area should be clean.
	• Storing, cooking and serving utensils should be kept clean	• Storing, cooking and serving utensils should be kept clean.
	• Separate kitchen with raised platform and store with proper shelves	• Display of information on menu, quantity of raw ingredients, quality of the food and usage of ration

(Contd…)

1	2	3
Infrastructure	• Kitchen and store rooms should be well ventilated, lighted, free from pests and rodents & must have favourable conditions for safe storage of food.	• Kitchen and store rooms should be well ventilated, lighted, free from pests and rodents & must have favourable conditions for safe storage of food.
	• Availability of proper drainage system, facility of functional toilets and access to safe drinking and cooking water is essential.	• Availability of proper drainage system, facility of functional toilets and access to safe drinking and cooking water is essential.
	• Fuel source should favourably be gas-line/LPG bottles & smokeless chullah.	• Fuel source should favorably be gas-line/LPG bottles & smokeless chullah.
Convergence	• Developing partnership with other developmental programmes, public and private organisations such as NGO, SHG, MHRD, MRD, MPR, SSA, MHFW, NRHM as a support to the MDMP for accomplishing its multi-level requirements	• Self Help Group, NGO, Local Youth Clubs, Municipality
Monitoring and evaluation	• National level, state level, district level, taluka level, school level, nodal agency, community participation	• District Education Officer, Nodal Officer and FCI District Manager along with school and community participation

INVESTMENTS FOR MID-DAY MEAL AT NATIONAL LEVEL

Documents of Ministry of Finance, Government of India (2008) indicate constant increase in the annual budget allocation for MDM. Realizing the immense potentialities of the programme, the government has materialized its priorities thereby, making concrete efforts towards improving MDM implementation. The current budget for year 2010-11 is Rs. 9912 crore.

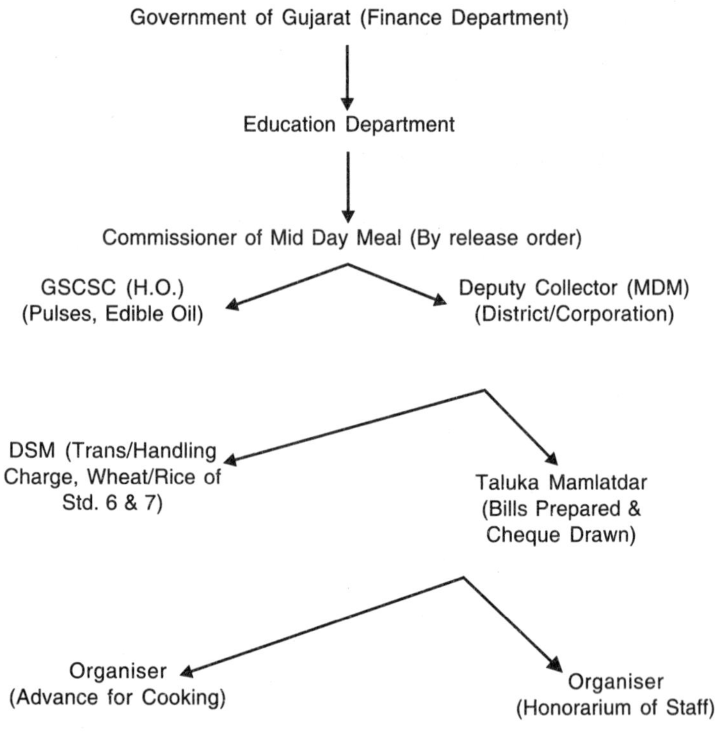

Fig. 3.2: Administrative Structure Under MDM at State Level

AWP-2007-08, GOG

ACHIEVEMENTS AND DRAWBACKS OF THE MID DAY MEAL PROGRAMME

Table 3.2

Achievements of the Mid-day Meal Programme Across the Country

Reference	Study Area	Outcome Indicator	Achievements
1	2	3	4
Sethi, (2008)	• Orissa	Enrolment	• Maximum enrolment was found in class 5 (52%) within 10 years after implementation of MDM
Dreze and Goyal, (2003)	• Rajasthan, Chattisgarh and Karnataka		• High enrolment for SC girls (42%) was observed in schools having MDM • Impressive rise in class 1 (14.5%), especially for girls, was found in Rajasthan (18%) as compared to Karnataka and Chattisgarh.
Laxmaiah et al (1999)	• Karnataka		• Higher enrolment (72%) in schools having MDMP as compared to non-MDM schools (68%) • Overall an impressive increase in enrolment was seen especially in the remote area and that too for girls
De et al (2005)	• Delhi	Demographic	• Reduction in population growth rate was seen in the tribal area of Orissa after MDM was initiated. This indicates that improved nutrition resulted in better survival rates and increased participation in school must have delayed the age of marriage.
Khera (2006)	• Summary of entire country		

(Contd...)

1	2	3	4
Dreze and Goyal, (2003)	• Rajasthan, Chattisgarh and Karnataka	Classroom hunger	• MDM showed an Overt in intensification of child under nutrition in many drought-affected areas • MDM has made a crucial contribution to food security in tribal areas
		Socialization	• Children from different class and caste sit together to have the MDM
De et al (2005)	• Delhi	Gender equity	• MDM minimize gender gap by improving attendance and enrolment of girls • MDM creates employment for women • 55% of increase in enrolment of girls was observed in Delhi due to MDM
Laxmaiah et al (1999)	• Karnataka	Attendance	• Improved attendance in schools having MDM (97.8%) than in non MDM schools (95%) was observed in Karnataka • Teachers (67.9%) in Delhi Corporation opined that MDM had improved attendance
De et al (2005)	• Delhi	Retention	• Higher retention in schools having MDM, with high proportion of girls (80.2%)
Sharma et al (2006)		Scholastic performance	• Proportion of students, who secured grade 'A' was marginally higher in MDM schools (13.1%) as compared to non-MDM schools (10.3%)
		Nutritional Status	• The per cent of children in normal category was marginally higher in MDM areas (3.0%) as compared to non-MDM areas (1.3%).

(Contd…)

1	2	3	4
De et al (2005)	• Delhi	Monitoring and Supervision	• Regular monitoring by 3rd party and the state level MDM officials helped to maintain basic infrastructural and hygiene standards among the MDM suppliers • 94.1% schools had some form of MDM committee in the Delhi Corporation, out of this 78.9% had members from the parent-teacher body, 24.1% had elderly citizens and only 13.9% had a health worker
CART (2007) Sharma et al (2006) Deodhar et al (2007)	• Rajasthan • Delhi • Ahmedabad	Quality service under Mid-day Meal	• 90% parents, 91% students and 99% teachers reported that the children were getting variety in menu • Grains allocated for MDM were found to be of good quality • The MDM was served regularly and punctually in Delhi Corporation • Most of the teachers (81%) reported the food quantity and quality to be adequate and acceptable • The MDM prepared in Ahmedabad was tasty and very good • The MDM staff in one of the 3 schools in Ahmedabad showed good personal hygiene and hygienic cleaning practices
		Health related activities Infrastructure and Logistics Safety against accidents	• In Rajasthan 88% students agreed that doctors and nurses have visited their schools for health check-up • Most of the schools (91.6%) received drinking water facility in the school out of which 73.4% had tap water facility • All the utensils were clean, in good condition and were of stainless steel. There was a separate and clean area for cleaning utensils • A fire extinguisher was observed in the kitchen of few schools in Ahmedabad

Table 3.3

Challenges Faced by the Mid-day Meal Programme Across the Country

Reference	Study Area	Outcome Indicator	Drawback
1	2	3	4
Dreze and Goyal, (2003)	• Rajasthan, Chattisgarh and Karnataka	Enrolment	• The register figures of beneficiaries were found to be inflated by teachers
		Socialization	• Indirect discrimination is observed as backward class cooks are not appointed
Khera (2006)	• Summary of entire country	Unsatisfied Staff	• Delay in reimbursing salary of the MDM staff was frequently noted in many states • Inadequate staff in proportion to the beneficiaries. In some areas (Rajasthan and M.P) independent staff is not appointed and thus teachers have to organize MDM • The appointed staff is overburdened with extra work accompanying the implementation of MDM. This affects their quality of work • MDM staff are given undefined and inadequate salary which creates incentive for corruption
De et al (2005)	• Delhi		• Low financial allocations for cooking cost thereby restricting the resources which affects quality and quantity of MDM prepared and distributed

(Contd...)

1	2	3	4
Robinson (2007)	• Madhya Pradesh		• Inadequate salary, extremely poor working conditions creates problem of retention of staff
			• Difficult and health hazardous working conditions for the staff
	• Rajasthan		• MDM personnel are not treated on par with other government employees, they are not entitled to monetary and miscellaneous benefits to which the government employees are eligible
CART (2007)	• Tamil Nadu	Health Concerns	• Most of the times MDM is prepared in unhygienic conditions due to poor infrastructure and lack of basic working conditions
Swaminathan et al (2004)	• Delhi		• Poor cleanliness, personal hygiene and food safety practices were observed among the food handlers in Rajasthan and Delhi
			• Poor cleanliness habits such as hand washing, plate washing, removal of shoes, trimmed nails, etc followed by children. In Delhi Corporation 35% children did not wash hand and their utensils before eating
Sharma et al (2006)	• Ahmedabad		• Poor pest management initiatives in the kitchen and store rooms caused high presence of pests and rodents
Deodhar et al (2007)	• Madhya Pradesh		• In Delhi Corporation the MDM is prepared in separate Food Supply Places (contract base) and these were located in interior areas, near open drainage and surrounded by unhygienic environments.
	• Bihar		• Waste disposal in most service units was not well organized and the garbage was not cleared frequently
Jain and Shah (2005)	• Mumbai		• The floor on which students sat to have their meal was quite dirty. Spilled food liquids from earlier days were not cleaned. Over all hygiene factor was missing in the practice as followed by children in Ahmedabad

(Contd…)

1	2	3	4
		Affects Teaching	• Due to lack of MDM staff, teachers have to organize and supervise and at times also get involved in cooking the MDM • 17% teaching time is lost in MDM related activities • Contrastingly 66.7% teachers in Delhi Corporation felt that MDM was cutting the study time • As observed in Ahmedabad, the teachers were involved in serving the cooked food which resulted in poor monitoring by them • Teachers have to get involved in collecting ration from the block and even buy vegetables and spices
		Infrastructure and Logistics	• Inadequate basic infrastructure for kitchen and store rooms that leads to unhygienic cooking and storing conditions (95% in Rajasthan) • Insufficiently ventilated, lighted and spacious kitchens and stores • The food service units in Delhi Corporation were not demarcated clearly and all the activities were undertaken in one or two small rooms. Also most of these units were inadequately lighted and ventilated • Inadequate cooking, storing and serving utensils. Most of the children (88.2%) brought their own utensils/tiffins from home • Old and worn out utensils with several dents that harbours harmful organisms; are being used • Hardly any drainage system due to which there is problem of stagnant water • Inappropriate fuel resources available (76% use firewood in Rajasthan)

(Contd…)

1	2	3	4
			• Water to be fetched from wells and hand pumps away from school vicinity • Untimely procurement of food grains • Poor toilet facilities • Poor coverage especially in tribal and remote areas • Manipulations in the recording of number of beneficiaries, amount of ration and vegetables used
		Monitoring and Supervision	• Lack of proper monitoring and supervision opens door to petty corruption, poor service delivery and poor hygiene • Teachers had only theoretical knowledge which affected the quality of monitoring • Stealing the allocated cash • Ration getting siphoned due to inadequate monitoring by the teachers and higher level officials • Corruption by local administration officers
Laxmaiah et al (1999) De et al (2005)	• Karnataka • Delhi	Quality services under mid-day meals	• Interrupted distribution of mid-day meal due to shortage of food stock (79%) • Uneven quantity of food was served to children due to lack of serving plates in most all the areas except T.N. • Lack of fresh vegetables were used • Food not cooked properly and not palatable • Presence of stones, insects, hair and other harmful foreign material • Problem of monotonous menu that lacks adequate vegetables is a serious concern

(Contd...)

1	2	3	4
Robinson (2007) Swaminathan et al (2004) Deodhar et al (2007)	• Madhya Pradesh • Tamil Nadu		• Dal/Sambhar served is half cooked and as thin as water, thereby hardly giving any protein and calories to the beneficiaries • Extremely poor quality of dry ration is supplied which often smells of decay and takes longer time to cook • MDM in Delhi Corporation do not follow any standard recipe • Some of the food grain sacks had noticeable amount of husk in the grains present at the MDM centre • The time allocated for serving and consuming MDM is too less especially in Ahmedabad • Nutritional evaluation of prepared food showed that iodine protein and calorie value were low, indicating lack of fruits and vegetables in the cooked MDM in Ahmedabad
Afridi (2005) Kapil and Sethi (2004)	• Ahmedabad • Delhi	Nutritional Status	• Prevalence of micronutrient deficiencies among children showed no significant difference between MDM and non-MDM schools • In New Delhi it was found that 52.5%, 45.0% and 11.1% children were underweight, stunted and wasted, respectively among 6-9 years old school age children
De et al (2005)	• Delhi	Community participation	• No PTA was involved • Lack of cooperation from teachers
Swaminathan et al (2004)	• Tamil Nadu	Supplementary benefits	• Little evidence on using MDM for object lessons in socialisation, hygiene, nutrition by teachers

(Contd...)

1	2	3	4
Sharma et al (2006) Kannyaian (2006)	• Delhi • Tamil Nadu	Safety against accidents	• Many schools in T.N. had kitchens in and/or near the class room which was not found to be a safe practice • In Delhi Corporation, the food serving units had 2-3 cylinders kept near huge burners or ovens which can cause accidents

Table 3.4

Achievements and Drawbacks of the MDMP in Gujarat

Reference	Area	Outcome Indicator	Achievements	Drawbacks
1	2	3	4	5
Kanani (1994)	Urban Vadodara	Attendance	• 77.7% of the teachers were of the opinion that MDMP increased attendance	
Nambiar and Roy (2010)	Tribal Vadodara			• A drop by 5.5% in the enrolment figures was recorded for the year 2010-2011 in the tribal region of Chotta Udepur taluka
Kanani and Elyayah (2008) Bakshi and Sharma (2008) Nambiar and Desai (2008) Nambiar and Gandhi (2008) Nambiar and S Nithya (2008)	Urban Vadodara	Sanitation	• Most of the cooking areas had satisfactory cleanliness • Most of the school had dustbin for disposing plate-waste • Cleanliness of most of the functionaries was rated as fair, thus showing an improvement from previous findings • 97% of the centres had closed drainage system • In urban Vadodara, as revealed by a recent study, utensils were washed before and after food was cooked	• Exceptionally few schools had poor cleanliness in the cooking area • Personal hygiene of functionaries was unsatisfactory • In half of the school, serving area was not swept and was dusty, flies were present, children did not wash hand before eating

(Contd...)

1	2	3	4	5
Nambiar and Patel (2010)	Rural Vadodara	Infrastructural facilities		• Due to lack of store room the ration as well as utensils were kept at the house of the incharge in rural Vadodara
Nambiar and Roy (2010)	Tribal Vadodara	Infrastructural facilities		• The tribal regions had gross infrastructural insufficiency such as inadequate number of • cooking and serving utensils, congested storerooms with shortage of space to store the grains
Kanani and Elyayath (2008) Bakshi and Sharma (2008) Nambiar and Desai (2008) Nambiar and Gandhi (2008) Nambiar and S Nithya (2008)	Urban Vadodara	Infrastructural facilities	• 46.7% mentioned about using a cooking gas cylinder. This shows some improvement in the MDM with time, as earlier studies showed contradicting results	• Schools observed in urban Vadodara had shortage of water • The kitchens were not equipped with gas connections • MDM centres had inadequate utensils (storing, cooking and serving utensils) • In urban Vadodara there was no proper storage facility for vegetables and spices • The serving area was found to be inadequate and unhygienic in most of the schools in urban Vadodara • The 7 MDM centres evaluated in urban Vadodara required more utensils and improved storing space for a better functioning

(Contd…)

1	2	3	4	5
Iyer and Dhaundiyal (2010)	Centralized Vadodara	Infrastructural facilities	• MDM in partnership with a NGO Akshay Patra had better infrastructure, machinery, storage facilities, manpower, sanitation, hygiene, food handling, menu, cooking process and transportation facilities than that school that were not supported by a NGO.	
Kanani and Elyayath (2008) Bakshi and Sharma (2008)	Urban Vadodara	Awareness about MDM	• 57% of the principal and 28% teachers were either supervising or monitoring MDM in their school.	• Most of the children and even parents were unaware about the rationale of MDM, and ate because either they were hungry, or because their friends were eating.
Nambiar and Desai (2008) Nambiar and Gandhi (2008)				
Nambiar and Desai (2008) Nambiar and Gandhi (2008)	Urban Vadodara	Management and logistics	• Incharges reported that hardly any cooked food was left over; this indicates proportionate usage of ration for cooking. • MDM in urban Vadodara, function for 210 days in a year, which is well within the suggestions given by NP-NSPE guidelines.	• Timing of serving MDM coincided with the lunch timings of the children, thus half of the children missed the home meals; either before coming to school or after going home. • Inadequate funds to meet the cooking cost

(Contd…)

1	2	3	4	5
Nambiar and S Nithya (2008)			• Using HSR, as a qualitative research methodology the multidepartment role of Vadodara Municipal Corporation in running the MDMP was studied and 9 departments were found to be involved; of which 7 departments showed a positive attitude for adopting interdepartmental approach towards betterment of the programme	• Calculations made on the usage of ration in urban Vadodara, reveals that in proportion to the number of children, deficit in ration usage was found. 28.5% cereals, 8% tuver dal and 2.5% oil was deficit.
Nambiar and Patel (2010)	Rural Vadodara			• Inadequate funds to meet salaries of staff • The incharges in rural Vadodara did not maintain any record regarding the ration usage
Nambiar and Roy (2010)	Tribal Vadodara	Teachers participation, Monitoring and supervision		• However contradictory results on the attitudes of the teachers towards MDMP were recorded by direct observations, since none of the teachers' monitored the preparation, storage, serving or records of MDM in all the 5 schools of ChhotaUdepur.

(Contd...)

1	2	3	4	5
Nambiar and Patel (2010)	Rural Vadodara			• The teachers in most schools did not take much interest in serving of MDM. • Teachers did not encourage children to eat the meals • Teachers were unaware of the MDM weekly menu as assessed in both urban and rural Vadodara. • Teachers were also unaware of their roles in MDM in rural Vadodara. • Contradictory to the scenario in urban Vadodara, the higher level officials had never visited any of the MDM centres.
Nambiar and Desai (2008)	Urban Vadodara		• The MDM staff and school authorities that Mamlatdars and Dept. of education come to inspect the MDM centres quite frequently. • Though 73.3%teachers revealed that MDMP improves the nutritional and health status and attendance.	

(Contd…)

1	2	3	4	5
			• Involvement of principals and teachers in MDM showed meagre improvement however not sufficient enough. 57% of the principal and 28% teachers were either supervising or monitoring MDM in their school.	
Nambiar and Roy (2010)	Tribal Vadodara	Quality of meal		• On comparing with the NP-NSPE guidelines, 2006 the quality of raw ingredients available in the tribal area was found to be sub standard and the personal hygiene practices of MDM staff workers was poor. • The average nutritive value of the MDM was 395 kcals and 10.48 g protein. • Menu served in the tribal regions of ChhotaUdepur was deficit in calories by 421 and had 12.2 gm of protein deficit
Nambiar and Patel (2010)	Rural Vadodara			• Poor quality of raw food supplied. • In rural Vadodara the food (ration and vegetables was not at all washed before preparing. • Only 2-3 monotonous vegetables were used in rural Vadodara (onion, Brinjal and potato)

(Contd…)

1	2	3	4	5
Kanani and Elyayath (2008) Bakshi and Sharma (2008) Nambiar and Desai (2008) Nambiar and Gandhi (2008) Nambiar and S Nithya (2008)	Urban Vadodara		• 83% Incharges stated that MDM was first tasted and only then served. • In majority of the schools in urban Vadodara, the meal was palatable and tasty. In most of the schools the weekly menu was followed. • The spices and condiments used in MDM were evaluated in laboratory and were found to be of excellent quality as there were standard products with AGMARK. • Among all the 7 schools evaluated, it was observed that MDM was served regularly and vegetable usage had improved by year 2009 in Vadodara city.	• Even the MDM served in urban Vadodara gave no micronutrient rich GLVs.

(Contd...)

1	2	3	4	5
Kanani and Elyayath (2008) Bakshi and Sharma (2008) Nambiar and Desai (2008) Nambiar and Gandhi (2008) Nambiar and S Nithya (2008)	Urban Vadodara	Community involvement	• Study states that effective use of innovative approaches such as Rapid Appraisal Survey method, Positive Deviance approach and Behaviour change communication can be inexpensive tools which can be used as developmental approach.	• Parents of MDM beneficiaries were largely ignorant (51%) regarding the objectives of the programme that it was supplement to the 3 main meals at home and not meant as substitution for a home meal.
Kanani and Elyayath (2008)	Urban Vadodara	Scholastic performance	• 52% girls felt that MDMP has improved their scholastic performance.	
Shah (2005) Sen and Kanani (2006) Kanani and Counsul (1990) Nambiar and S Nitya (2008)	Urban Vadodara	Nutritional Status	• Impact of vegetable intervention in MDM revealed that the prevalence of under nutrition significantly decreased in the experimental group. • MDM that was augmented with vegetables showed a reduction the prevalence of night blindness and Conjuctivalxerosis after augmenting.	• The study has reported 34% (according to Must et al standards) and 19% (according to Agarwal standards) prevalence of under-nutrition in urban Vadodara. • Study revealed that the prevalence of anaemia was found higher (67%) in adolescent girls.

(Contd…)

1	2	3	4	5
				• 25-50% of adolescent girls had ocular signs of vitamin A deficiency. • 60% underweight and 68% stunting was prevalent among the children. • 73% suffered from night blindness and more that 75% suffered from anaemia and vitamin C deficiency.
Iyer and Dhaundiyal (2010)	Centralized Kitchen		• Children consuming meals provided in schools supported by AkshayaPatra, showed that the mean rise in weight (1.19 Kg Vs. 590 gm) and height (1.26 Vs. 1.15 cm) was significantly higher than the non-NGO supported school. • Prevalence of WAZ, HAZ and BMIZ reduced marginally by 1.9%, 0.46% and 5.33% respectively in the AkshayaPatra collaborated school. Thus partnership with such NGO can help improve the meal quality and quantity of MDM.	

(Contd…)

1	2	3	4	5
Nambiar and Roy (2010)	Tribal Vadodara			• Though most of the students of 6th and 7th standard were consuming MDM for more than 3 times a week (81.3%) since past 6-7 years, the NSA datarevealed the prevalence of severe thinness to be 44.7% in tribal area of ChhotaUdepurtakula of Vadodara. • Along with poor nutritional status, the presence of clinical signs of IDA such as pallor in nails (30.9%), conjunctiva (35.3%), tongue (12.1%), palm (19.3%), breathlessness (6.3%) and koilonychias (0.5%) were also recorded.

4 Mid Day Meal Scenario in Schools of Rural Vadodra

The present section discusses the detailed methodology and results of a study planned with the broad objective to monitor and evaluate the Mid Day Meal Scheme schools of Rural Vadodara and assess the functioning of MDM in comparison with the NP-NSPE guidelines (2006) guidelines.

The specific objectives of the study were:

- To assess the impact of MDM programme on: enrolment, attendance, category rate and gender and MDM beneficiaries.
- To assess the Mid Day Meal kitchen, School Infrastructure and Nutritive value, Quality and Quantity of the meal served under MDM.
- To assess the Knowledge, Attitude and Practices of the Teachers, Students and MDM Staff regarding Mid Day Meal Scheme.

METHODS AND MATERIALS FOR THE STUDY

Prior to initiate the survey, permissions were obtained from various government departments such as MDM office (Gandhinagar), MDM office (Vadodara) and Education department (Vadodara). Consent letters from the Education Department were obtained for co-operation from the school authorities during the data collection period. The further content describes about various parameters observed and measured during the survey. This study was funded by the Government of Gujarat-Department of education, MDM section.

SCHOOL DETAILS – TECHNIQUES AND FINDINGS

The details of the children's enrolment, attendance, gender and caste were gathered using the secondary data which were collected from the school's annual registers. Both current and past year's records were obtained from the attendance records maintained by teachers.

Secondary information consists of sources of data and other information collected by others and archived in some form. These sources include government reports, industry studies, archived data sets, and syndicated information services as well as the traditional books and journals found in libraries. Secondary information offers relatively quick and inexpensive answers to many questions and is almost always the point of departure for primary research (Stewart and Kamins, 1993).

Schools of rural Vadodara (obtained from MDM Office) were enlisted (n=161) and 10 schools were selected for the survey (Table 4.1). Medium of instruction in all the schools was Gujarati and the school timings were 11:00 am to 5:00 pm on weekdays and 7:30 am to 11:00 am on Saturdays. Out of the 10 schools, 7 were co-ed, 2 were only girls and 1 was only boys school. In all the schools, MDM was served between 2-3 pm during the recess. Figure 4.1 is the map describing the location of the selected schools.

IMPACT OF MDM ON ENROLMENT, ATTENDANCE AND GENDER

Enrollments Details

Table 4.2 shows the enrollment details obtained from the registered school records and compared between 2 academic sessions of the year.

Table 4.1

Details of the 10 Schools Surveyed in Rural Vadodara

School Code No.	School Name	Medium of Education	Type of School			School Shift
		Gujarati	Girls	Boys	Co-ed	Afternoon
I	Chaani Girls school	√	√	–		√
II	Kalali Primary school	√	–	–	√	√
III	Sevasi Primary school	√	–	–	√	√
IV	Kapurai Primary school	√	–	–	√	√
V	Dashrath Primary school	√	–	–	√	√
VI	Bajwa Primary school	√	–	–	√	√
VII	Undera Primary school	√	–	–	√	√
VIII	Ankodia Primary school	√	–	–	√	√
IX	Bhayli Girls school	√	√	–	–	√
X	Sokhda Primary school	√	–	√	–	√

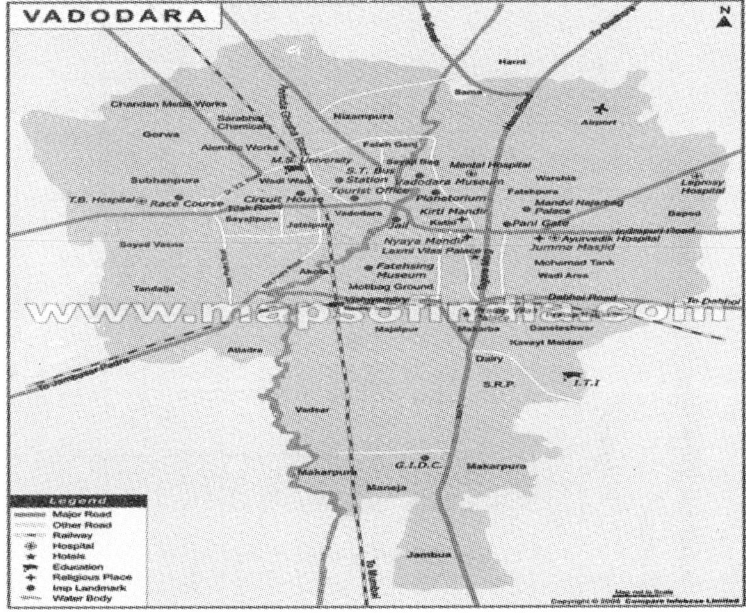

Fig. 4.1: Map of Vadodara City

The total number of children enrolled in standards 1-7 in all schools range from 180-750 as per the data. The number of students enrolled showed an increase in 40 per cent (n=4) of the schools (maximum in School VI, Bajwa by 11.2 per cent and minimum in School X, Sokhda by 2.5%). Students enrolled in 7th standard in all schools varied from as low as 21 students in school VI (Bajwa) to as high as 119 students in school VII (Undera) which had three sections. However the overall figures reveal a 16.5 per cent decrease in enrollment.

This is contrast to an increase in the enrollment reported by several investigators in various parts of India. Studies conducted in Western India by CART (2007) in Rajasthan surveyed 211 schools reported increase in enrolment and retention in 64 per cent of the schools, enrolment of girls had increased in 58 per cent of the schools. In Southern India findings of Laxmiah et al (1999) revealed that the number of children enrolled in MDM schools was higher (72%) as compared to non-MDM schools (68%) in Karnataka.

Table 4.2
Number of Students Enrolled in Schools of Rural Vadodara
(April v/s September)

School Code No.	Students Enrolled in Each Standard														Total		
	1st		2nd		3rd		4th		5th		6th		7th				
	P	C	P	C	P	C	P	C	P	C	P	C	P	C	P	C	%
I	39	38	40	45	75	66	66	72	69	80	65	63	62	67	416	431	3.6↑
II	25	28	35	28	32	31	27	30	30	22	40	26	18	32	207	197	4.8↓
III	22	37	44	27	33	43	31	37	26	31	46	27	24	45	226	247	9.3↑
IV	50	47	52	50	75	53	64	72	58	64	60	59	81	57	440	402	8.6↓
V	65	57	83	55	75	89	88	70	94	86	34	78	59	30	498	465	6.6↓
VI	50	75	52	41	63	56	37	67	29	32	24	25	30	21	285	317	11.2↑
VII	70	66	97	68	80	103	118	81	124	122	126	125	122	119	737	684	7.2↓
VIII	17	19	23	18	22	22	37	22	28	37	32	33	28	33	187	184	1.6↓
IX	52	27	31	55	51	29	44	48	39	37	32	30	51	31	300	257	14.3↓
X	33	37	35	35	61	36	33	57	28	28	27	24	22	28	239	245	2.5↑
Average																	-16.5

Note: P = Previous year, C = Current year, % = Per cent increase or decrease in enrolment

Caste and Gender Details

Figure 4.2 reveals that overall 66.9 per cent (n= 2295) students enrolled in 10 schools under the study were of lower caste (SC, ST and OBC) as compared to 33.1 per cent (n= 1134) students which belonged to the general category. Among these students, the number of girls enrolled (55.1%) was greater than the number of boys (44.9%).

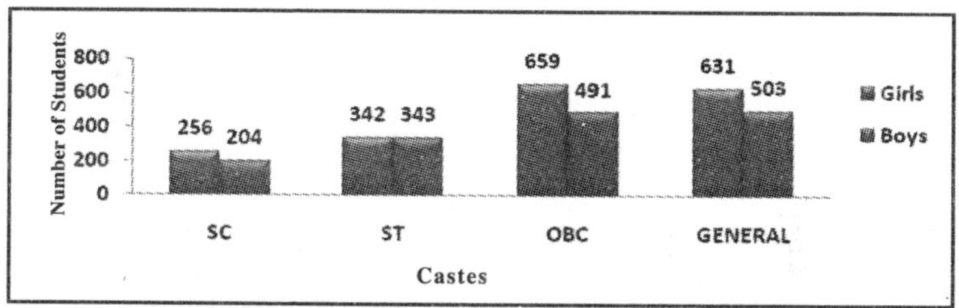

Fig. 4.2: Categorization of Students according to the Caste and Gender in 10 Schools of Rural Vadodara

Several investigators have reported increase in enrollment of lower caste children in schools. Jain and Shah (2005) revealed a marked increase in the case of SC and ST children (43%). The rise in the enrollment of girls was 38 per cent out of this the increase in enrollment of SC and ST girls were 41 per cent. Sethi (2002) also reported that the greatest impact of the programme was seen on the S.T. and girls' enrolment by 42 per cent each.

The objective of MDM is to encourage poor children, belonging to disadvantaged sections to attend school more regularly and help them concentrate on classroom activities. It also reduces gender gap in education by enhancing female attendance in schools. The overall gender gap in enrolment at the primary stage has dropped to 4.6 percentage points and that at the upper primary level has reduced to 8.0 percentage points in 2005. Girls' enrolment at the primary stage increased from 28.1 per cent in 1950-51 to 46.7 per cent in 2004-05. At the upper primary stage, girls' enrolment rose from 16.1 per cent in 1950-51 to 44.4 per cent in 2004-05 (Rath, 2008).

Education is not just about literacy and numeracy, it can also give people knowledge about health, hygiene, nutrition, in addition to basic skills or trades which enable them to feed themselves and their families. Increasing the percentage of educated women in a community can greatly reduce childhood hunger. The number of years a woman attended school can reduce the likelihood that her child will be malnourished by up to 40 per cent (Sisulu, 2006).

Under Sarva Shiksha Abhiyan a provision of expenditure up to Rs. 15 lakh per year can be used for taking up innovative interventions relating to girls' education and education of SC/ST children (www.ssa.nic.in).

The targeted provisions for girls under Sarva Shiksha Abhiyan include: Free textbooks to all girls upto class VIII, Separate toilets for girls, Back to school camps for out-of-school girls, Bridge courses for older girls, 'Innovation fund' per district for need based interventions for ensuring girls' attendance and retention, girls only schools at upper primary level within the State policy (www.ssa.nic.in).

MDM Beneficiaries

The results on the comparison between the registered students v/s the MDM beneficiaries reveal a range 34.1 per cent to 95.9 per cent (minimum in school I, Chaani and maximum in school VII, Undera). The average number of MDM beneficiaries in 10 schools was 66.4 per cent (Figure 4.3).

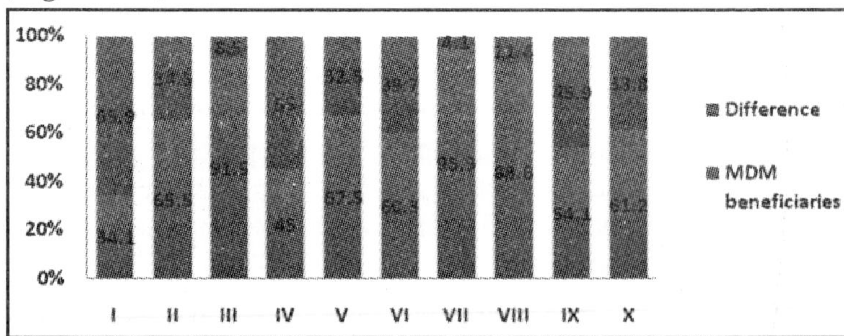

Fig. 4.3: Registered Students v/s Actual MDM Beneficiaries in All Schools as per Records

Study done in North India by Sharma et al (2006) revealed that the average number of children consuming MDM on a regular basis was 75.5 per cent and the reasons for the rest of the children not consuming MDM was mainly the food not being tasty, children not being allowed by their guardians/ parents to eat MDM or utensils not brought on the day MDM was served.

The actual coverage of children in primary and upper primary schools by the programme in 2008-09 in Gujarat was 93 per cent and 100 per cent respectively. The number of children who participated in the programme as on 30-Sep-08 in primary section were SC (8%), ST (26%), OBC (51%), Other (12%) and AIE (2%) and in upper primary section it was SC (10%), ST (23%), OBC (52%) and Others (15%) (MDM AWP & B 09-10).

Attendance Rate

To assess the impact of MDM programme, the attendance records of one month of the current academic year were obtained. Since the students of 7th standard formed the sample size of the present study, details of their records revealed that students were regular in attending school. A variation of 67.5 per cent-98.8 per cent was observed, with minimum attendance in school II, Kalali and maximum in school III, Sewasi (Figure 4.4).

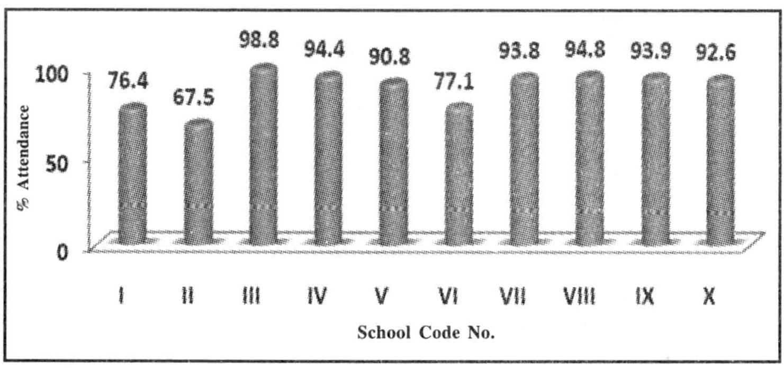

Fig. 4.4: Average Attendance Rates of Students of 7th Standard in Selected Schools

Similar reports on attendance in schools offering MDMP by Rana et al (2005) revealed that increase in attendance of ST girls (>8%) was higher than that of the ST boys in West Bengal. Laxmiah et al (1999) reported higher attendance in MDM schools (97.8%) than Non-MDM schools (95%). This indicates that MDM is one of the significant incentives for children to attend the school regularly.

Highlights

- Among the children enrolled 66.9 per cent were from SC, ST and OBC category as compared to 33.1 per cent of general category.
- The number of girls enrolled was greater than the number of boys i.e. 55.1 per cent v/s 44.9 per cent in all the 10 schools.
- Only 66.7 per cent of the children were consuming the mid day meal from the total number of children enrolled in all schools.

The average attendance rate of students in all schools was 88 per cent.

INFRASTRUCTURE OF SCHOOL AND THE MID DAY MEAL KITCHEN

Qualitative research techniques such as spot, direct and participatory observations were used to obtain information on infrastructure of MDM and School, hygiene practices of MDM staff and meal preparation procedures by staff.

Qualitative Research

It is a field of inquiry applicable to many disciplines and subject matters. Qualitative researchers aim to gather an in-depth understanding of human behaviour and the reasons that govern such behaviour. The qualitative method investigates the why and how of decision making, not just what, where, when. Hence, smaller but focused samples are more often needed, rather than large random samples. Qualitative research, broadly defined, means "any kind of research that produces findings not arrived at by means of statistical procedures or other means of quantification" (Strauss & Corbin, 1990).

Observations

Rather than relying solely on people's self-reports of events, or physiological or institutional data, many researchers prefer to make their own observations (Neill, 2006).

1. Spot observation

The method of "spot observations" has been used to characterize the activities of groups of specific age, sex, and occupation within particular societies. A "spot" record captures by observation the activities of all individuals present at the moment of entry into the household, and, by subsequent interview with those present, the activities of those not in view.

The data are then coded in standard activity categories and then the data are processed to determine the percentage of time spent on any particular class of activity by any individual or class of individuals. One simply calculates the number of instances of that activity as a percentage of all activities recorded (i.e. as a percentage of the number of visits) (Rogoff, 1978).

2. Direct observation

Direct observation is an underused and valuable method for collecting evaluation information. "Seeing and "listening" are key to observation. Observation provides the opportunity to document activities, behaviour and physical aspects without having to depend upon peoples' willingness and ability to respond to questions (Taylor and Steele, 1996).

3. Participatory observation

The term "participant observation" refers to naturalistic, qualitative research in which the investigator obtains information through relatively intense, prolonged interaction with those being studied and first hand involvement in the relevant activities of their lives. The primary data are typically narrative descriptions (i.e. field notes) based on direct observation, informal conversational interviews and personal experience, although quantitative and more formal, structural data can also be collected through participant observation (Levine et al, 1980).

1. Kitchen

A comparison of the MDM infrastructure with the NP-NSPE guidelines reveals that out of ten schools, 70 per cent (n=7) of the schools had a separate kitchen shed in the school premises, however, in 20 per cent (n=2) of the schools cooking was done in open space and in 10 per cent (n=1) school it was done outside store room provided by the school. All the schools had a decentralized kitchen. In 40 per cent (n=4) of the schools, raised cemented platforms were made for cooking and firewood was used as a cooking fuel in all except for one school where LPG cylinder was used for cooking which was brought by the MDM incharge from her own resources (Figure 4.5).

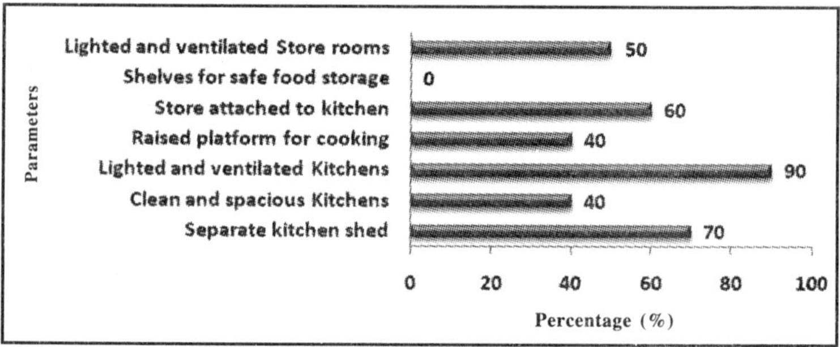

Fig. 4.5: Infrastructure of Kitchen and Stores in Selected Schools of Rural Vadodara Conforming to the NP-NSPE Guidelines, 2006

About 70 per cent (n=7) of the school kitchens had cemented floors and walls which kept them clean and free from insects and pests. Adequate serving utensils were provided in 80 per cent (n=8) of the schools but the cooking utensils were inadequate and were very old. The eating plates were provided to the children in only 20 per cent (n=2) of the schools by school authorities and MDM incharge.

2. Storage of raw materials

All the schools had a storage room for food grains within the school premises. The store rooms should be attached to the kitchen according to the guidelines but in Rural Vadodara, only 40 per cent (n=4) of the schools had store rooms away from the kitchen areas they were generally a classroom which was converted to a store.

None of the store rooms had shelves, 5 schools had good ventilation, in 30 per cent (n=3) schools, grains were adequately stored in drums covered with lids while in other schools they were stored in the gunny bags which had a chance of spoilage by the insects. Flies and pests (especially rodents) were present in 70 per cent (n=7) schools (Figure 4.5).

The salt and spices were adequately stored in air tight containers in 30 per cent (n=3) and 50 per cent (n=5) schools respectively. Vegetables are generally bought on daily basis by the staff and sometimes potatoes, tomatoes, onion etc were stored in 30 per cent (n=3) of the schools either in gunny bags or utensils or kept open on the floor. Cottonseed oil was provided from the government (fortified with Vitamin A and D), but was kept in open tins which could lead to loss of the fortified vitamins. Iodized salt was used in all the schools, however, open packets and improper storage conditions may lead to loss of iodine present in it.

Thus, based on the NP-NSPE guidelines (2006) for kitchen and storage areas, overall only 30 per cent and 20 per cent schools conformed to the guidelines respectively (i.e. for Kitchen- separate area, clean and spacious, lighted and ventilated and adequate serving utensils and for store room- Attached to kitchen and well lit and ventilated).

Several investigators have reported the infrastructural facilities of MDM in various states of the country.

Rana et al (2005) reviewed that 60 per cent of the schools had separate kitchen shed and only 4 schools had rooms to store food and space to serve the meal to the children. The scenario was poor in Rajasthan as reported by CART (2007) only 5 per cent schools had a kitchen shed, 36 per cent schools had separate store rooms, 76 per cent schools used firewood, 14 per cent used gas and 10 per cent used kerosene as a cooking fuel and 83 per cent of the cooks confirmed that they have sufficient utensils for MDM preparation. In Karnataka NIPCCD (2007) revealed that ventilation of the kitchens was far from satisfaction and in 60 per cent schools LPG was used and in remaining kerosene oil and firewood was used.

In Udaipur district, Blue (2005) reported the cooks in 4 villages out of 8 villages, prepared meals at their own houses and carried it to school for distribution, in 3 villages meals were prepared over an outdoor wood fire in open area and in one village meals were prepared over a makeshift fire place in a small room within the school building and in 2 schools secondary class students used to prepare and serve the meal to the primary children. None of the schools had permanent kitchen sheds. Only 2 schools had enough dishes for all primary students. Teachers and cooks in 2 out of 8 schools reported irregular delivery of both wheat and funds.

The MDM centers of Urban Vadodara had better infrastructure than rural areas about 75 per cent of the kitchens and store rooms were well ventilated and LPG gas bottles and gas pipelines were used in as a cooking fuel in 84 per cent of the centers (Nambiar and Gandhi, 2008).

Our studies reveal that though a contingency for building kitchen sheds and utensils is available from the State Government, further improvement in infrastructure of the kitchen and store rooms should be initiated as a reason of safety issues. The food prepared either in open air or in a makeshift thatched shed have a danger of food being contaminated resulting in severe accidents. Shelves or cupboards in the storerooms should be made for proper and safe storage of raw materials. Pest control measures should be taken to provide safe food to the children and regular testing of Mid Day Meal for microbiological content should be done. The use of smokeless chulhas should be encouraged as firewood produces huge quantity of smoke and ash which are hazardous to health and pollute the environment (CART, 2007).

In the year 2008-09 an amount of Rs 5581 Lakhs for 9303 kitchen-sheds was released by the GOI (Government of India) for construction of kitchen sheds to Gujarat State, Rs 3790 Lakhs was handed over to Sarva Shiksha Abhiyan to construct 6318 kitchen sheds, out of targeted units and Rs. 335.35 lakhs were provided for the purpose of procurement of kitchen utensils for 6,707 MDM Centres (MDM AWPB 09-10). Though funds are allocated for improving the infrastructure facilities and the number of units targeted, are not achieved. Thus co-ordination and inspection of the funds should be administered at various levels.

3. Procurement of grains

The food grains (cereals, pulses and fortified wheat flour) and oil were provided by the Food Corporation of India. At the end of each month, the MDM incharge had to submit the record of used and left over ration to the MDM office and based on these records, receipt for the procurement of grains for next month was given. The grains were received on time in all the schools and no such incidence had occurred wherein the stock of grains was nil and the MDM was not cooked for the day.

The MDM incharge maintains the stock records in all the schools and only in one school (School III, Sewasi) the principal monitored the usage of ration where as in other schools the stock was not monitored by the school principal and teachers. The food grains were received from the ration shop on time in all schools. Weighing balances for measuring the procured grains were not available in any of the schools.

Results on the procurement of grains were reported by CART (2007) in a study in Rajasthan which revealed that only 23 per cent of the schools were able to receive food grains after getting them weighed before delivery, out of which 12 teachers incharge of MDM reported that underweight food grain bags were received. And 89 per cent of the schools received food grains on time and in others it was delayed for about 6-15 days and more.

4. Serving details

In 70 per cent (n=7) schools service area was unclean, food was served in open ground. In 60 per cent (n=6) schools, students did not pray before eating and teachers did not monitor and maintain discipline while the children were having food and did not motivate children to finish food (Figure 4.6). In most of the schools food was being served by elder students to all the children and not by the helper or cook.

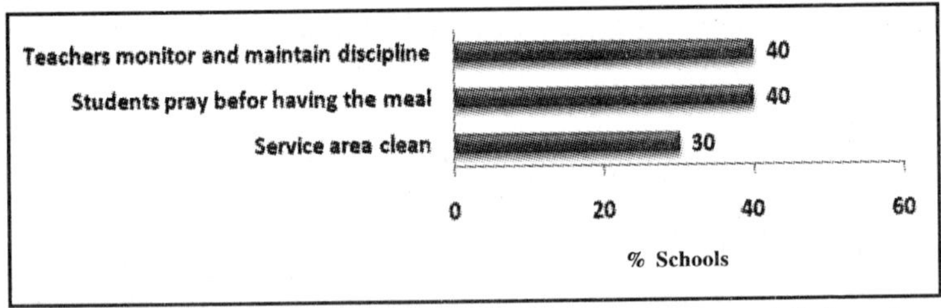

Fig. 4.6: Serving Details of the MDM in Selected Schools

Few departmental studies done on evaluation of MDMP by Nambiar and Desai (2009), (Nambiar and Gandhi, 2008) have revealed that separate and properly constructed serving area were available only in 19 per cent schools of urban Vadodara, while in 81 per cent schools, the food was served in corridors or open playground with no cover or shed.

Regular maintenance of the school environment is essential to prevent deterioration over time. Whitewashing and painting, roof and site drainage, maintenance of the water and sanitation facilities, site cleanliness and greenery are a recurring requirement with respect to school buildings. SSA provides funds for maintenance which are as follows: upto Rs. 5000 per year per school, Rs. 7500 is provided for schools having classroom more than 3 and Rs. 4500 for the schools having upto 3 classrooms (Department of School Education and Literacy, 2007).However, since there is no linkage between the monitoring or the education and MDM officials, overall improvement is lacking in these schools.

5. Water and Toilet facilities

India is the 2nd most populated country in the world, it has been a challenge to universally provide safe drinking water and sanitation facilities in India.

Department of Drinking Water Supply in the Ministry of Rural Development, Government of India has got provision under Accelerated Rural Water Supply Programme (ARWSP) to cover rural schools with drinking water facility. Further, Total Sanitation Campaign (TSC) provides toilet and urinals for rural schools (www.ssa.nic.in). The budget for Department of Drinking Water Supply in Rural areas for the year 2010-11 is Rs. 10583.78 crores (DDWS, 2010-11).

However, our results reveal that the drinking water facility was available in all the schools except for one school (School IV, Kapurai). Village tank water was available in 90 per cent (n=9) schools and in other well water and Hand pump water was used for cooking and drinking purposes. In 2 of the schools the helper had to go far away (< ½ kilometer) to fetch water.

In Kapurai village, there was a major problem of water availability; the whole village used to get water from corporation through water tanker supplied once in a day. The water tanker came either early in the morning or in evening. Therefore the school did not receive corporation water and thus the MDM staff had to get the well water which was near to the school. The quality of well water was suspicious as the water turned yellow in colour few minutes after fetching. In Chaani School few students were not having MDM reason behind this was unsafe water as it was polluted by rodents and insects which used to fall in the tank which was not covered from the top.

Separate toilet facilities were available for boys and girls in schools but none of them were functional as water was not available. In one school there were eight toilets and in others 3-4 toilets were present. Sanitation of the toilets was very poor, leading to unhygienic conditions which may cause infectious diseases among the children. Already the health status and immunity levels of the children in rural areas are low and if there are unsanitary and unhygienic surroundings, the health status of children would further deteriorate. Therefore the sanitation of the toilets is an important issue that needs to be taken care of and steps should be taken by the schools and Education department in improving the conditions.

As per census 2001, only 36.4 per cent of the total population of the country had toilets within their households. This was even less in rural areas i.e. 21.9 per cent, and out of this, only 7.1 per cent households have toilets with water closet. Another issue is lack of safe drinking water and sanitation facilities in all schools especially in rural areas, which has been a matter of concern. The consequences that result from the given situation are Diarrhoea, Typhoid, dysentery, gastroenteritis, hepatitis A, intestinal worms and malaria that continue to kill, debilitate and contribute to the high rates of malnutrition among young children in the country (School Sanitation and Hygiene Education, 2004).

As mentioned earlier though SSA provides, funds, the conditions of the toilets and water supply reveal another story. A number of studies conducted reflected a contribution of these facilities in access and retention of children. There is almost a direct correlation between the drop-out of girls at upper primary level and the availability of sanitation facilities within the school. Provision of drinking water and toilet facilities is one of the basic requirements in a school. In spite of large scale provisioning of schooling facilities there is still a large gap which is unlikely to meet through the SSA funds. Hence convergence with other schemes, especially of the Ministry of Rural Development, Government of India is crucial to achieve 100 per cent coverage of such facilities.

Several studies have shown inadequate drinking water and toilet facilities. A survey conducted in South India found that 51.9 per cent of primary schools did not have usable toilets and a further 11.5 per cent did not even have the infrastructure and 42 per cent of primary schools in the state have no separate toilets for girls (Chakravarthy, 2010). Studies in Western India by CART (2007) reviewed that 88 per cent of the schools (n=211) in Rajasthan had drinking water arrangements, 82 per cent of the schools had urinals, 61 per cent schools had toilets, out of which only 62 per cent and 21 per cent were being used respectively as there was no provision of water. A study in North India reported that nearly in every school, there were dirty toilets. In some cases, the toilets were just locked up and children were encouraged to go in the open. Sometimes this area could be just behind the classrooms where children ate their food (De et al, 2005).

6. School kitchen gardens

Only two of the schools had medicinal plants and none of the schools had grown vegetables in their premises. Though the schools had open space for growing kitchen gardens but they were not developed by school authorities.

The schools having compound wall and not having compounded wall or fence faced similar problems of cattle's entering the premises and eating away the plants and possibility of theft of vegetables and plants by the village people. Thus because of these reasons kitchen gardens were not developed in schools.

School gardens have several interrelated objectives like:

- Increasing the relevance and quality of education for rural and urban children through active learning and through introduction of agriculture and nutrition knowledge and skills, including life skills, into the curriculum.
- Providing school children with practical experience in food production and natural resource management, which serve as a source of innovation they can take home to their families and apply in their own household gardens and farms.
- Improving school children's nutrition by supplementing school feeding programmes with a variety of fresh micronutrient and protein-rich products, and increasing children's knowledge of nutrition, to the benefit of the whole family. (FAO, 2004)

Thus initiatives should be taken by the education department and school authorities to develop a kitchen garden which is not only beneficial in terms of nutrition to the children but also helps children to obtain environmental knowledge and skills.

NUTRITIVE VALUE, QUALITY AND QUANTITY OF THE MEAL SERVED UNDER MDM

Nutritive Value Evaluation of the MDM

For calculating the nutritive value of the meal, the utensils used by the MDM incharge at schools for measuring the food grains while taking out the ration were measured with the help of Salter scale and bathroom scale for knowing their actual weights. Then on the basis of the quantity of the utensils and its frequency used in getting the ration for a particular day was calculated from which the amount of ration obtained per child was evaluated by dividing the total number of beneficiaries. Based on the raw weights nutritive value of the meal was calculated using NIN standards and these amounts were compared with the NP-NSPE guidelines for ration allocation per child and approximate nutritive value per child.

Quality Assessment of Raw Materials

Raw ration like grains and spices were collected from all the 10 schools and were evaluated by visual examination. The parameters assessed were presence of dirt, dust, stones, bran and insects.

The center (Supreme Court of India in 2001) has recommended a provision of hot cooked meals with minimum 450 Kcal and 12 g proteins per child per day. The grains provided per child by the Center is 100g rice/wheat, the state additionally provides 20g dal and 10g oil per child. Gujarat Government has introduced a new venture of introduction of fortified wheat flour (FWF) in entire Gujarat State since 25th Sept 2009.

A special MDM menu has been formulated by the MDM section, Government of Gujarat, to be implemented across the state. Since the introduction of FWF, changes in the menu have been suggested, however, on the spot observations revealed that this menu is not followed strictly in all the schools (Table 4.3).

Table 4.3

Menu Followed Before and After Incorporation of the Fortified Wheat Flour in the Schools of Rural Vadodara

Days	Menu Before Implementation of the Fortified Wheat Flour as per MDM office Records	Menu After Implementation of the Fortified Wheat Flour (From 25th September 2009)	Actual Menu Observed
Monday	Khichdi+ vegetable	Khichdi+ vegetable	Khichdi+ vegetable
Tuesday	Kansar+ vegetable	Kansar+ vegetable/ Roti + vegetable	Kansar+ vegetable/ Meethi lapsi/ Tikho lot
Wednesday	Dal Bhaat	Dal Bhaat	Dal Bhaat
Thursday	Dal Dhokadi	Fada lapsi + vegetable/Roti + vegetable	Fada lapsi + vegetable/ Meethi lapsi/ Tikho lot
Friday	Pulao Bhaat	Dal Dhokadi	Dal Dhokadi
Saturday	Fada Lapsi	Pulao Bhaat	Pulao Bhaat

Prior FWF the menu had rice based meals for three days (Khichdi + vegetable, Dal Bhaat and Pulao Bhaat) and wheat based meals for three days a week (kansar+ vegetable, Dal Dhokadi and Fada lapsi) which was replaced by FWF after its introduction.

However actual spot observations, record checking and key informant interviews reveal that the MDM served to the children differs from the actual menu provided through government. The Kansar+ vegetable is substituted with only boiled and spiced FWF recipes such as "Tihko lot" and "Meethi lapsi" (Table 4.4). Acceptable recipes such as rotis/bhakhri or thepla along with vegetable were not prepared in any of the schools.

Table 4.4

Food Items Prepared Out of Three Types of Cereal Foods

Type of Cereals	Food Items
Rice based	Khichdi-shak, Dal bhaat, Pulao Bhaat
Wheat based	Fada lapsi
Fortified wheat flour based	Kansar-shak, Dal dhokadi, Tikho lot, Meethi Lapsi

The micronutrients added in the 50 gm of wheat flour are shown in the Table 4.5.

Table 4.5

Micronutrients Present in 50 gm of Fortified Wheat Flour

Micronutrients Present in Fortified Flour	50% of the RDA
Calcium	225 ug
Iron	7.5 mg
Iodine	50 ug
Zinc	5 mg
Vitamin A	200 ug
Riboflavin	0.5 mg
Ascorbic acid	20 mg
Folic acid	20 ug
Vitamin B_{12}	0.5 ug

However, the acceptability of the fortified flour recipes was very low among the children. The flour after cooking turned dark in colour and was not palatable to consume. For making Chapatti the required utensils were not provided in the schools therefore it was not prepared in the menu and it is more time consuming and would require more staff members (Table 4.6) Also in dal dhokadi served in the schools, dhokadi has to be prepared but due to lack of utensils it was rolled on the floor or on the lid. Dhokadi rolled on the floor of the kitchen is an unhygienic practice followed by the staff which should be modified.

Proper facilities should be provided for storage of fortified floor. Shelves or elevated platforms should be made in the store rooms. In one school we observed that though the fortified flour bags were kept on benches, they were infested by the rodents.

Therefore, along with improvement in storage facilities pest control measures should be taken to avoid infestation of raw materials. Cooks in some of the schools had a practice of sieving the fortified flour before cooking to make it more refine. This practice of the cooks, removed the bran particles of wheat from the flour which is a nutritious part of the flour.

Thus, the staff should be given training and education regarding the safety and hygiene practices while cooking and new recipes of fortified flour should be incorporated in the menu and correct preparation procedures should be taught to the staff which would make nutritious and palatable food items in the MDM.

1. Adequacy of ration in MDM

Food grains (wheat and rice) for 1 to 5th standard are provided by the Central Government and for 6 to 8th standard the State Government provides the grains. The Dals and oil are allotted by the State Government to all the classes and salt, spices and condiments are brought by the incharge from local market for which the cost is given by the State government. Food grains and oil are supplied from the Food Corporation of India (FCI) go-downs. Vegetables are purchased on daily basis by the incharge and there is no fixed vendor from whom the vegetables are purchased.

Though the center suggests provision of 100g cereals, 20g dal and 10g oil per child per day (NP-NSPE, 2006), the Government of Gujarat guidelines suggests only 5g oil per child per day. The menu for rural Vadodara has been modified by the MDM wherein changes for amount of oil have been

Table 4.6
Positive and Negative Aspects of Fortified Wheat Flour

Menu	Infrastructure Facilities	Requirements	Perceptions		
			Students	Teachers	MDM Staff
Dal Dhokadi	Not adequate	Roti making equipments not present	Palatable	Palatable	Palatable, inadequate utensils and storage facility for fortified flour.
Meethi Lapsi/ Kansar	Adequate infrastructure facilities	Big utensils and ladle present	Not palatable	Not palatable, less amount of sugar/jaggery and oil is used.	Not palatable, Children like more of spicy foods.
Tikho Lot	Adequate infrastructure	Big utensils and ladle present	Not palatable	Not palatable, turns dark in colour and becomes sticky, less oil is used.	Not palatable, Flour should be more refined.

done (Table 4.7). The Rural Vadodara MDM office have also modified the usage of red gram (tuver) dal based on the menu suggests provision of 40g dal three times a week instead of 20g daily for 6 days. However, our results reveal that only chana dal was supplied to the schools.

Table 4.7

Ration Allocation of the Weekly Menu as per the MDM in Rural Vadodara

Days	Menu	Ingredients	Ration (gms)
Monday	Khichdi+ vegetable	Rice	100
		Chana Dal	40
		Oil	3
		Vegetables	50
Tuesday	Kansar + vegetable/ Roti + vegetable	Fortified flour	100
		Oil	7
		Vegetables	50
Wednesday	Dal-Bhaat	Rice	100
		Chana Dal	40
		Oil	3
Thursday	Fada Lapsi + vegetable/ Roti + vegetable	Fada	100
		Oil	7
		Vegetables	50
Friday	Dal-Dhokadi	Fortified flour	100
		Chana Dal	40
		Oil	7
Saturday	Pulao-Bhaat	Rice	100
		Oil	3
		Vegetables	50

Moreover, there were no weighing scales present in schools for measuring the grains for cooking as per the number of MDM beneficiaries. The incharges used either a bucket or a vessel of 1 kg, 2 kg or 5 kg to quantify ration. Though measured utensils were used for taking out the ration, a deficit was seen which could be due to the manipulations made by the incharge.

Figure 4.7 shows the average ration used by the schools. The average ration allocated per child was 73 gm of cereals (Rice, Wheat and Fortified wheat flour), 33 gm of pulses (Chana dal) 20 gm of vegetables and 3.3 gm of oil.

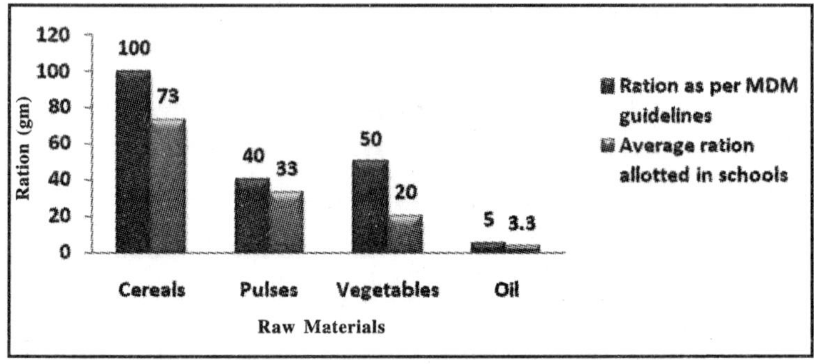

Fig. 4.7: Average Ration Allotted in Schools per Child

Since serving plates were provided only in two schools, there was no proper serving size which was monitored/child/day. On average children get one serving (200ml) of the meal daily in schools depending on their tiffin box. Some students even ate on paper sheets or newspapers if they did not bring a tiffin box. Thus quantification of MDM was not equal for all children.

A comparison of the total ration utilized v/s actual allocation by the Government, in 10 schools revealed that there was a deficit of 27 per cent of cereals, 17.5 per cent of pulses, 60 per cent of vegetables and 34 per cent of oil.

Since MDM provides Rs. 9440 crores of budget for the schools which includes money for purchase of utensils, serving plates have to be procured in order to ensure that the children are consuming the stipulated ration provided by the Government. It is also suggested that standardized serving spoons should be used and the staff should be trained in serving equal amount of the meal to the children.

Similar findings of ration deficit were reported by several investigators, 40 and 70 gm of cooked food was provided in Madhya Pradesh (Jain and Shah, 2005), 150-200 gm per child/

day was provided in Delhi (Sharma et al, 2006), 80 gm of Bulgar wheat and 5 gm soya oil supplied 303 Kcal and 7.2 gm protein instead of 330 Kcal and 7-12 gm protein in Karnataka (Laxmiah et al, 1999). The quality of food provided in schools of Delhi was poor. Dal or subzi was watery, few beans of rajma and a lot of gravy were observed in Rajma and the vegetable pulao had no vegetables. The amount of food given to each child was no more than two ladles of food. It appeared to be more of a snack than a meal (De et al, 2005). In rural Vadodara (Nambiar and Desai 2009) a difference in the amount of ration used for cooking and the actual amount of ration being consumed was observed, which indicated that the values of beneficiaries were being manipulated and the ration was being siphoned which resulted in the menu being deficit in calories, proteins and micronutrients in all schools.

2. Nutritive value of the MDM

According to the average ration allotted per child in the schools, the average nutritive value was calculated which shows about 421Kcal energy and 12.2 gm proteins were provided from the menu (Figure 4.8). Thus the nutritive value almost met the guidelines. But according to the norms the students of 6-7th standard should obtain about 700 Kcals and 20 gm proteins which did not convene from the meal.

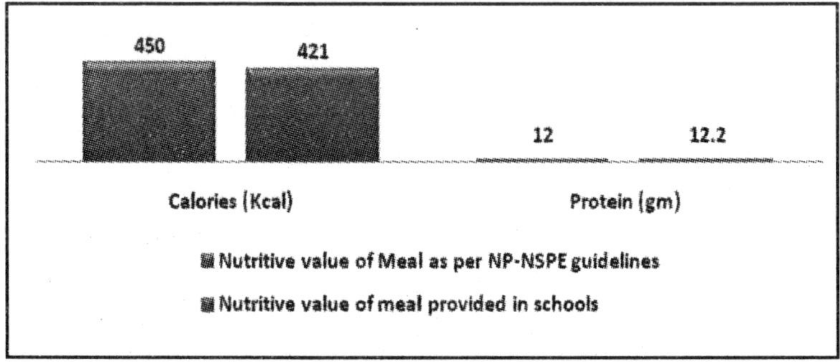

Fig. 4.8: Comparison of the Nutritive Value of the Meal Served in Schools with the NP-NSPE Guidelines, 2006

The energy requirements of adolescents tend to parallel their growth rate and these increased requirements are met through their appetite. The nutritional requirements of young people are influenced primarily by the spurt of growth that occurs at puberty. The peak of growth is generally between 11 and 15 years for girls and 13 and 16 years for boys (www.eufic.org).

The Figure 4.9 shows the per cent RDA of children for calories and proteins met through the meals. The mid day meal provided in the schools gives about ¼ and 1/3 of the RDA for calories and protein to 6-9 years old students whereas in elder students of 10-15 years it provides less than ¼ of the RDA for calories and protein. As per the norms 1/3 of the RDA of children should be met through Mid Day Meal in schools but predominantly they get about ¼ of the RDA for calories and protein.

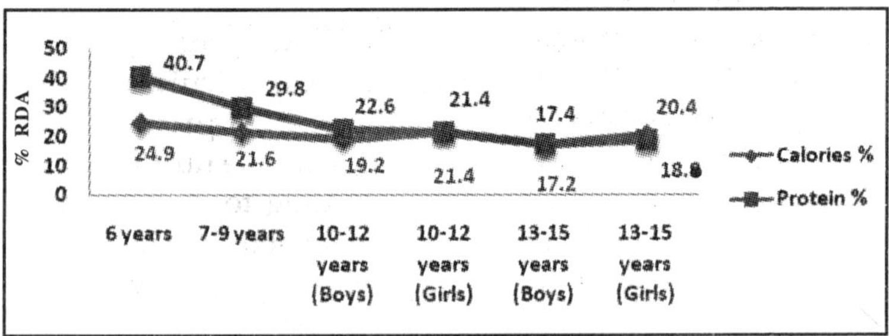

Fig. 4.9: Per cent RDA for Calories and Protein of the Children met Through MDM

In rural areas generally the children of lower socio-economic status are coming to the school thus the income of the family affects their calorie intake at home and if inadequate quantity of food is given to these children in schools than undernourishment would result. Local community institutions/associations such as Gram Panchayats, Village Education Committees and Parent teacher Associations should be involved in the activities of MDM. Methods such as performance based incentives and award competitions should be conducted to enthusing and building capacities of these institutions so that they can play a vital role in education and overall development of their children. The quantity of food grains delivered to the schools need to be weighed to ensure that there are no leakages. In schools of U.P. a committee had been constituted at Gram Panchayat level to supervise day to day cooking at school level which involved Gram Pradhan as President, two gentlemen and two ladies who were parents of the children studying in the school and the head master of the school (Wizarat, 2009).

FOOD SAFETY, SANITATION AND HYGIENE PRACTICES IN MDMS

The terms food safety and food quality can sometimes be confusing. Food safety refers to all those hazards, whether chronic or acute, that may make food injurious to the health of the consumer. Quality includes all other attributes that influence a product's value to the consumer. This includes negative attributes such as spoilage, contamination with filth, discolouration, off-odours and positive attributes such as the origin, colour, flavour, texture and processing method of the food (www.who.int).

Food safety is an essential public health issue for all countries. Food borne diseases due to microbial pathogens, biotoxins, and chemical contaminants in food represent serious threats to the health of thousands of millions of people. Food borne diseases not only significantly affect people's health and well-being, but they also have economic consequences for individuals, families, communities, businesses and countries. These diseases impose a substantial burden on healthcare systems and markedly reduce economic productivity. Poor people tend to live from day to day, and loss of income due to food borne illness perpetuates the cycle of poverty (www.who.int).

The sanitation and hygiene practices followed by the MDM incharge, cook and helper and of students were observed.

1. Practices followed by the Staff and Students

In 20 per cent (n= 2) of the schools waste was disposed off outside school premises whereas in other schools waste was disposed inside school premises near the kitchen area. Figure 4.6 shows the practices followed by the staff in washing grains and vegetables prior to cooking.

In only 20 per cent (n=2) schools the utensils were washed before beginning the food preparation. Dustbins were present in 20 per cent (n=2) of the schools but were not used by the Staff for disposing waste materials. There are no fire and safety measures provided for the staff in any schools and none of the staff follow a practice of adding salt at the end of cooking.

2. Hygiene practices of the staff

The hygiene practices of the staff like trimmed nails, trimmed hair, clean and tidy clothes etc. were observed. In 80 per cent (n=8) of the schools, staff had trimmed nails, clean and tidy clothes and all had trimmed hair. In only two of the schools the staff used to wash hands prior to handling food and in one school the MDM incharge was chewing tobacco.

3. Hygiene practices of the students

The sanitation and hygiene practices followed by the students were observed and are presented in Figure 4.10. Only the students of 30 per cent schools used to wash hands and 60 per cent washed plates prior eating the meal.

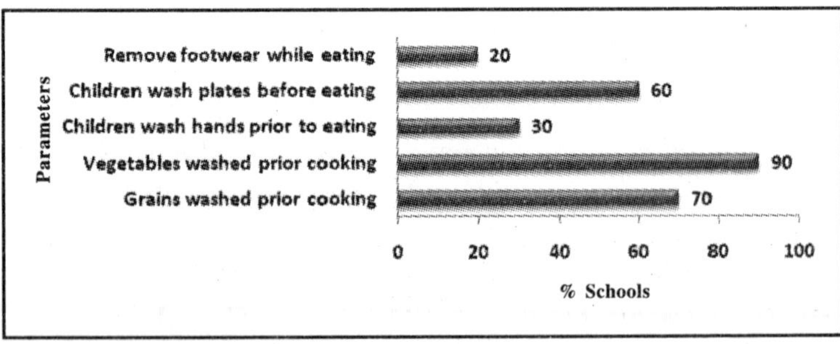

Fig. 4.10: Sanitation and Hygiene Practices Followed by MDM Staff and Students

A study on 121 schools have reported that about 56 per cent centers in urban Vadodara disposed waste in VMC vans daily, 17 per cent gave the waste to cattles to feed and 28 per cent disposed out of the school campus. All staff members had trimmed nails, hair tied neatly, wore clean and tidy clothes and 28 per cent of the staff wore footwear in the kitchen and store area (Nambiar and Gandhi, 2008). An investigator in Delhi reported that none of the teachers insisted the children to wash their hands before the meal (De et al, 2005). CART (2007) suggested that the hygienic behaviour among students should be encouraged. Only 5.5 per cent of the surveyed students did not wash hands before having MDM, while 86 per cent of students wash hands with only water and 95 per cent of the students did not cut their nails timely.

Nambiar and Desai (2009) reported that 57 per cent MDM staff showed an improvement in the safe food handling and proper food storage practices by providing training of staff through an integrated action plan in schools of urban Vadodara. Thus, the staff should be trained in safe and hygienic handling of foods, behaviour change communication strategies should be adopted to make the MDM staff aware of the correct procedures during cooking, serving, waste disposal and cleaning and storing of the utensils and raw materials. The teachers should educate and train the students in following hygienic habits and maintaining personal hygiene.

4. Quality of Food grains

According to the NP-NSPE guidelines 2006, FCI will issue food grains of best available quality, which will in any case be at least of Fair Average Quality (FAQ).

The quality of food grains was assessed for the presence of dirt, dust, stones, excess bran and the uniformity in size and shape. Presence of dirt and excess bran in grains was found in 90 per cent (n=9) schools and insects were present in 50 per cent (n=5) of the schools. The spices used in cooking had AGMARK on the label except for one school and all spices were free from insects (Figure 4.11). Iodized salt (Brands:

"Sheetal salt", "Jay salt" etc) was used in all the schools but their storage condition was improper in 7 schools, they were either stored in polyethylene bags or loose jars. The cotton seed oil (Brands: *"Gokul" and "Tirupati"*) was supplied to all the schools from the MDM center. They were not stored in air tight containers but kept in their original oil tins which had their lids closed loosely.

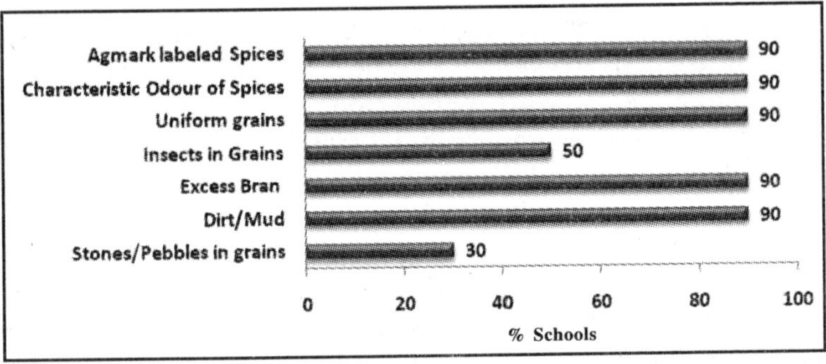

Fig. 4.11: Quality of Food Grains and Species Used for Cooking in Schools of Rural Vadodara

In West Bengal poor quality of food was supplied and mostly one single item was prepared i.e. khichdi, this made some of the children to skip the lunch at school (Rana et al, 2005). 97 per cent of the students rated the meal to be of average quality in a study in Rajasthan by CART (2007).

Highlights

- In two of the schools cooking was done in open space and in one school it was done outside store room, while in remaining seven schools there was a separate kitchen shed built in the school premises.
- In store rooms, none of the schools had shelves for safe food storage.
- In half of the schools there was a difficulty in procuring water for cooking and drinking as the helpers had to get the water from a distance from the school.
- The schools had separate toilet facilities for boys and girls but in none of the schools they were functional.

- The quantity of food served to the children does not match the guidelines. The average ration allotted per child was cereals 73 gm, pulses 33 gm, vegetables 20 gm and oil 3.3 gm in the schools.
- Only two of the schools provided serving plates to the children. They get unequal amount of food as per their size of plates and Tiffin boxes.
- The meal provided 421 Kcal and 12.2 gm protein per child/ day which did not met the guidelines for Upper primary children.
- The acceptability of fortified wheat floor was poor among the students. It turned dark in colour on cooking and was unpalatable to consume.
- MDM staff does not follow safe food handling practices, in only two of the schools the staff had a practice of washing hands prior to handling food.
- The hygiene habits of students were also poor. Students in only three of the schools washed hands prior to having food, in six of the schools the students washed plates before having the meal.

Positive Deviant Practices

Positive Deviance (PD) is an approach to personal, organisational and cultural change based on the idea that every community or group of people performing a similar function has certain individuals (the "Positive Deviants") whose special attitudes, practices/ strategies/ behaviours enable them to function more effectively than others with the exact same resources and conditions (Seidman and McCauley, 2003).

The positive deviant practices of the MDM staff, Teachers and Students were observed in the schools. The positive attitudes and behaviours like cleaning and washing of grains before cooking, proper storage of raw materials, monitoring of serving of MDM by teachers, variety of vegetables used in the meals etc (Table 4.8).

Table 4.8

Positive Attitudes and Behaviours of MDM Staff, Teachers and Children Observed in Schools

Parameters	Best Practices
MDM infrastructure	Kitchen area was clean and was well lit and ventilated in 4 schools.
	Adequate storage of grains in drums in 3 schools and spices stored in air tight containers in 5 schools and salt also stored in air tight containers in 3 schools.
	Dustbins were used in 2 schools.
Sanitation and hygiene of staff	80 per cent staff had trimmed nails and wore clean and tidy clothes.
	30 per cent wore footwear in kitchen and store area.
	20 per cent had a practice of washing hands prior to handling food.
	96.7 per cent did not smoke or chew tobacco.
Safe food handling practices by staff	Grains were washed prior cooking in 7 schools.
	Vegetables were washed prior cooking in 9 schools.
	Utensils were washed before being used for cooking in two schools.
	Waste was disposed off outside school premises in 2 schools.
	Kitchen floor was washed everyday in 4 schools.

(Contd…)

Parameters	Best Practices
Involvement of Teachers in the programme	Serving of the MDM was being monitored by teachers in 4 schools.
	Ration usage was monitored in one school by the principal.
	Plates were provided to the children in two schools by school authorities.
Hygiene practices of Children	Children washed hands before having the meal in 3 schools.
	Plates were washed before having the meal in 6 of the schools.
	Children had a habit of removing footwear while having the food in 2 schools.
Incorporation of nutritious recipes	A variety of vegetables like bottle gourd, brinjal, beet root, potato, tomato and cabbage were incorporated in the recipes which made it highly palatable in one school.

On the basis of these behaviours positive deviance initiatives, behaviour change communication strategies and training should be given to improve the knowledge, attitude, awareness and participation of the staff, teachers and students in the schools.

Positive practices in the Mid day meal were observed in some states of the country. In Karnataka active participation of the teachers was observed. They taste the meal before serving it to the children and ensure that the children wash their plates and keep it clean. They also educated the children about the cleanliness and hygiene. School Development Monitoring Committees (SDMC) were developed which include the head teacher of the primary school, elected members of the village government and parents of children. This committee actively participates in the development of the school infrastructure, donating land, additional items like cooker, mixie, wash basin, grinder etc for the Mid day meal programme. The schools had developed kitchen garden within their compound. Aqua guard facility was available in the schools (Srinivas K, 2008).

In schools of Rajasthan the Principal were also responsible for ensuring that the cook was supplied with calculated amount of food grains as per the attendance of the children and that the food was cooked properly. One teacher in all of the schools under the SDMC (School Development Monitoring Committee) was entrusted with the responsibility of buying fruits for the children which were being provided once a week. In all of the schools children were asked to clean their hands before and after having food. There were either taps or hand pumps in the school. In one of the school's there were posters showing the appropriate method of cleaning the hands displayed on the school notice board. The food was being served in the steel plates. Almost all the children were made to sit on the mats spread in front of the corridor of the class rooms and the children were being given a second serving also (Kaushal S, 2009).

The crucial and important sub-systems of the School feeding programmes are:

1. the technology consisting of quality and quantity of the food provided;
2. the delivery system comprising of components like transport, storage and mode of distribution/feeding whether take-home or on the spot feeding; and
3. the acceptability of the programme by the target group.

As any of the factors approaches zero, the effectiveness of the programme also approaches zero. No matter how perfect the blend or supplement from the point of nutrient content may be, if the delivery system is inadequate or the food is not acceptable to the population due to factors of taste or culture, the effectiveness of the programme approaches zero. Even under conditions of perfect delivery system and universal acceptance of quality food, if the quantity is inadequate for the group, the effectiveness is bound to be sub-optimal (Rao N.P).

Thus, all the aspects of the programme i.e. the quality, quantity, infrastructure, service etc. should be taken care off for the Mid Day Meal programme to be successful. The positive and negative deviant practices are shown in the following pictures given below.

Positive Deviant Practices	Negative Deviant Practices
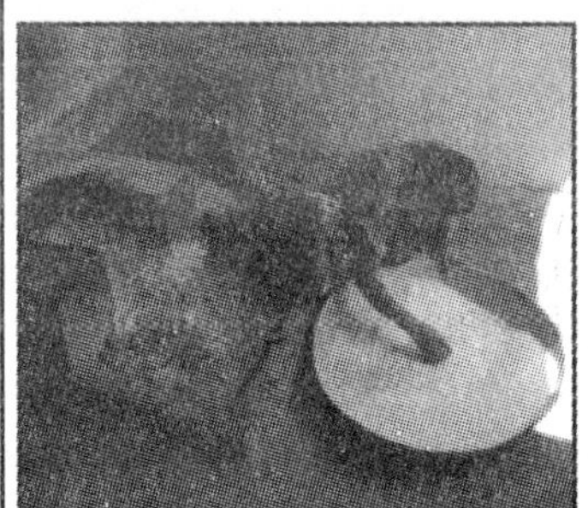	
Plate 1 Grains cleaned in a Utensil	*Plate 2* Grains kept on Flour while Cleaning

Positive Deviant Practices	Negative Deviant Practices
 *Plate 3* Variety of Vegetables Used in MDM	 *Plate 4* Potatoes and Onions mostly Cooked in MDM
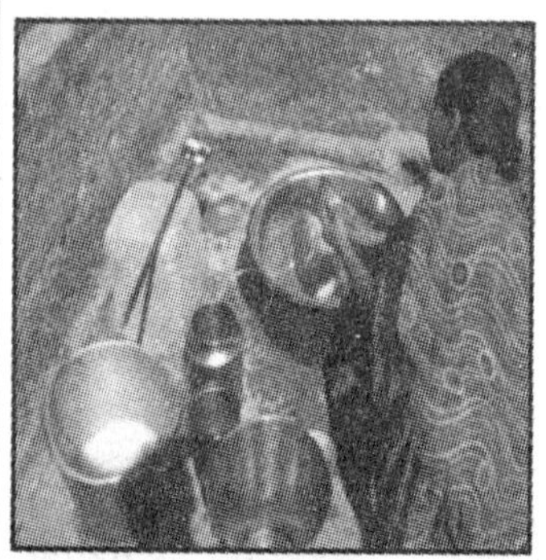 *Plate 5* Separate Washing Area Outside Kitchen	 *Plate 6* No Separate Washing Area Present

Positive Deviant Practices	Negative Deviant Practices
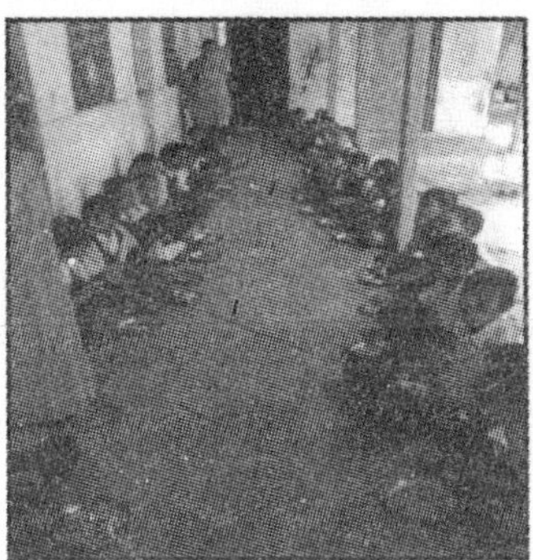 *Plate 7* Children having meal in shade	 *Plate 8* Children sitting in open ground for Meal which would become inconvenient during summer and monsoon
 *Plate 9* Grains stored in Drums	 *Plate 10* Grains stored in gunny bags

Positive Deviant Practices	Negative Deviant Practices

Plate 11
Spices stored in Air tight containers

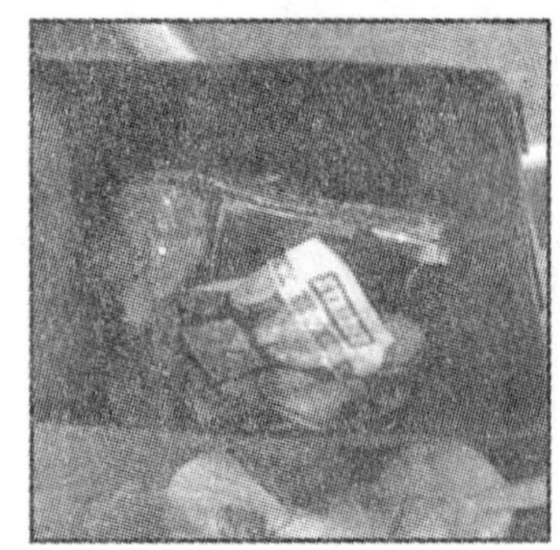

Plate 12
Spices stored in polyethylene bags

Plate 13
Fortified flour stored Above from the ground

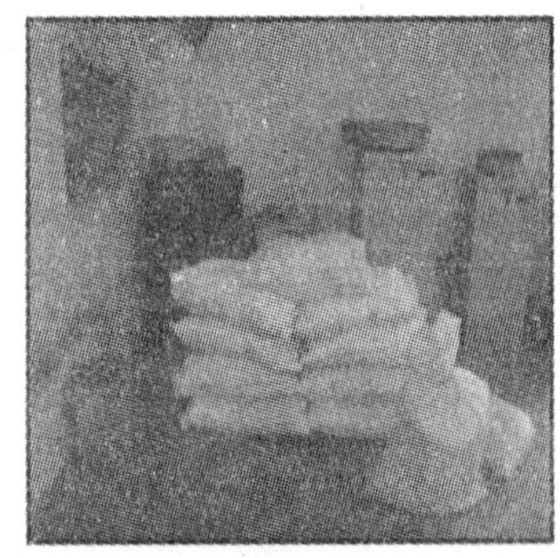

Plate 14
Fortified Flour stored on floor

Positive Deviant Practices	Negative Deviant Practices

Plate 15 Students pray before having the meal	*Plate 16* Students do not pray before having the meal
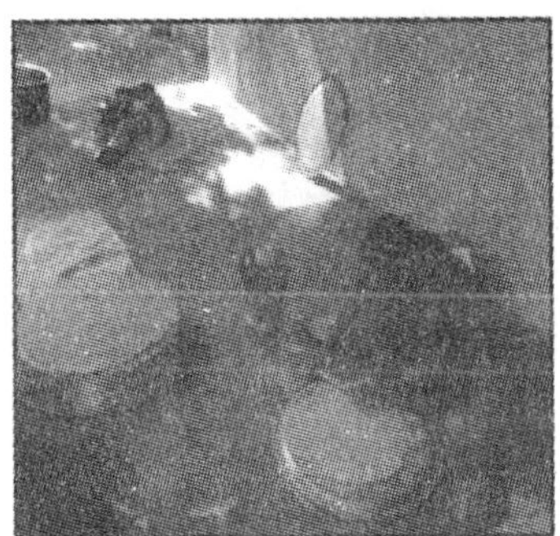	
Plate 17 Dhokadi (Dal Dhokadi) Rolled on utensil	*Plate 18* Dhokadi (Dal Dhokadi) rolled on floor

QUESTIONNAIRE SAMPLES

Sample 1: Record sheet for collecting information of the enrolled students and the MDM beneficiaries' actual registered figure of students

Standard	Caste								Total
	SC		ST		OBC		General		
	Girls	Boys	Girls	Boys	Girls	Boys	Girls	Boys	
1st									
2nd									
3rd									
4th									
5th									
6th									
7th									
Total									

Sample 2: Actual registered figure of MDM beneficiaries

Standard	Caste								Total
	SC		ST		OBC		General		
	Girls	Boys	Girls	Boys	Girls	Boys	Girls	Boys	
1st									
2nd									
3rd									
4th									
5th									
6th									
7th									
Total									

Sample 2: Checklist for spot observation of the infrastructure facilities in the school and the mid-day meal centre

Form No.

Date:
School Number and Address:
Medium of instruction: Gujarati/Hindi/Other
School shift: Morning/Afternoon

Sr. No.	Parameters	Indicators	Findings	Observations
1.	Water facility	Source of water	(a) Tap water (corporation) (b) Hand pump (c) Well (d) Other	
2.	Toilet facility	Total number of toilets	(a) One (b) Two (c) Three (d) Other	
		Number of functional toilets	(a) All (b) Other (c) None	
		Separate toilet for boys and girls	(a) Yes (b) No	
		Level of cleanliness	(a) Very clean (b) Clean (c) Average (d) Dirty (e) Very dirty	

Sample 3: Infrastructure of the kitchen and store area

Sr. No.	Parameters	Indicators	Findings	Observations
1.0	Kitchen	Location	(a) In class room (b) Separate (c) Other	
1.1		Type	(a) Centralised (b) Semi-centralised (c) Decentralised	
1.2		Clean and spacious	(a) Yes (b) No	
1.3		Ventilation channels (windows)	(a) Good (more than 2) (b) Average (only 2) (c) Poor (less than 2)	
1.4		Adequate source of natural light	(a) Yes (b) No	
1.5		Flooring	(a) Cemented (b) Concrete (c) Muddy (d) Tiled (e) Other	
1.6		Walls	(a) Cemented (b) Concrete (c) Muddy (d) Tiled (e) Other	
1.7		Raised platform for cooking	(a) Yes (b) No	
1.8		Fuel	(a) Lpg cylinder (b) Lpg pipeline (c) Firewood (d) Kerosene	
1.9		Adequacy of cooking utensils	Tapela (a) Yes (b) No Kadhai (a) Yes (b) No	

(Contd…)

Sr. No.	Parameters	Indicators	Findings	Observations
1.10		Adequacy of serving utensils	(a) Yes (b) No	
2.0	Store Room	Location	(a) Attached to kitchen (b) Away from kitchen (c) In classroom (d) Other	
2.1		Provision of shelves for storage of grains	(a) Yes (b) No	
2.2		Ventilation channels (windows)	(a) Good (More than 2) (b) Average (Only 2) (c) Poor (Less than 2)	
2.3		Adequate source of natural light	(a) Yes (b) No	
2.4		Floor	(a) Cemented (b) Concrete (c) Muddy (d) Other	
2.5		Walls	(a) Cemented (b) Concrete (c) Muddy (d) Other	

Sample 4: Evaluation of the Mid-Day Meal Activities

Kitchen work management

Sr. No.	Parameters	Indicators	Findings	Observations
1.0	Raw material procurement and management	Grains (Wheat, rice, pulses)	(a) Centre (b) State (c) Local	
1.1		Spices and condiments	(a) Centre (b) State (c) Local	
1.2		Vegetables	(a) Centre (b) State (c) Local	
1.3		Oil	(a) Centre (b) State (c) Local	
1.4		Maintenance of records	(a) Yes (b) No	
1.5		Provision of weighing scales	(a) Yes (b) No	
1.6		Weighing of the food procured	(a) Yes (b) No	
1.7		Teachers monitor usage of ration	(a) Yes (b) No	
2.0	Storage	Grains	(a) Gunny bags (b) Drums (c) Other	
2.1		Spices and condiments	(a) Air tight container (b) Loose jars (c) Polyethylene bags (d) Other	

(Contd...)

Sr. No.	Parameters	Indicators	Findings	Observations
2.2		Vegetables	(a) Baskets (b) Polyethylene bags (c) Other	
2.3		Oil	(a) Air tight container (b) Plastic/ glass jar (c) Other	
2.4		Oil is vitamin A and D fortified (provided by Govt.)	(a) Yes (b) No	
2.5		Use of iodized salt	(a) Yes (b) No	
2.6		Presence of flies and pests in storeroom	(a) Yes (b) No	
2.7		Water storage	(a) Tanks (b) Drums (c) Utensils (d) Buckets	
3.0	Pre-preparation	Washing of grains	(a) Yes (b) No	
3.1		Source of water for washing grains	(a) Tap water (corporation) (b) Handpump (c) Well (d) Other	
3.2		Washing of utensils	(a) Yes (b) No	
3.3		Source of water for washing of utensils	(a) Tap water (corporation) (b) Handpump (c) Well (d) Other (e)	

(Contd…)

Sr. No.	Parameters	Indicators	Findings	Observations
3.4		If yes, then utensils are washed with	(a) Water only (b) ·Soap and water	
3.5		Washing of vegetables	(a) Yes (b) No	
4.0	Preparation	Time of initiation of cooking		
4.1		Fire and safety measures for staff	(a) Yes (b) No	
4.2		Time at which cooking process ended		

Post Preparation Information

Sr. No.	Parameters Assessed	Indicators	Findings	Observation
5.0	Serving details	Serving time		
5.1		Presence of teachers while food is being served	(a) Yes (b) No	
5.2		Students wash hands before eating	(a) Yes (b) No	
5.3		If yes, students wash hands with	(a) Only water (b) Soap and water (c) Other	
5.4		Students pray before eating	(a) Yes (b) No	
5.5		Students remove foot ware while eating	(a) Yes (b) No	
5.6		Vessels	(a) Own (b) Provided by school	

(Contd…)

Sr. No.	Parameters Assessed	Indicators	Findings	Observation
5.7		Serving area	(a) Dining hall (b) Corridor (c) Classroom (d) Other	
5.8		Teachers motivate children to finish food	(a) Yes (b) No	
5.9		Teachers maintain discipline while children are eating	(a) Yes (b) No	
5.10		Frequency of serving	(a) Once (b) Twice (c) Thrice (d) Other	
5.11		Eating area	(a) Dining hall (b) Corridor (c) Classroom (d) Other	
6.0	Washing	Washing of utensils	(a) Only with water (b) Water and soap (c) Other	
6.1		Frequency of washing floor	(a) Daily (b) Every alternate day (c) Once a week (d) Other	
6.2		Floor is washed with	(a) Only with water (b) Water and soap (c) Other	
6.3		Students wash hands after eating food	(a) Yes (b) No	
6.4		If yes, students wash hands with	(a) Only water (b) Soap and water	

(Contd...)

Sr. No.	Parameters Assessed	Indicators	Findings	Observation
7.0	Disposal	Use of dustbins	(a) Yes (b) No	
7.1		Different bins for dry & wet waste	(a) Yes (b) No	
7.2		Waste disposal	(a) Within school premises (b) Outside school premises (c) Corporation vans	

Sample 5: information and hygiene of the staff

Sr. No.	Parameters	Indicators	Numbers (n)	Findings
1.1	Staff members	In charges		
1.2		Cooks		
1.3		Helpers		
1.4		In charge teachers		
2.1	Hygiene of staff	Trimmed nails	(a) Yes (b) No	
2.2		Trimmed hair	(a) Yes (b) No	
2.3		Use of footwear in the kitchen and store area	(a) Yes (b) No	
2.4		Clean and tidy clothes	(a) Yes (b) No	
2.5		Wash hands prior to handling food	(a) Yes (b) No	
2.6		Smoke or chew tobacco	(a) Yes (b) No	
2.7		Wipe sweat with a handkerchief	(a) Yes (b) No	

Sample 6: Assessing the nutritional value of MDM

Total No. of Children	Days	Menu	Ingredie Nts	Amount (gm/ml)	Serving Size (gm/ml)	Amount Served per child	Calories (kcals)	Protein (gm)
	Monday							
	Tuesday							
	Wednesday							
	Thursday							
	Friday							
	Saturday							

Sample 7: Evaluation of the quality of raw materials

Parameters	Indicators	Findings	Observations
Whole wheat	Foreign matter	Stones/pebbles (a) Present (b) Absent Dirt/Mud (a) Present (b) Absent Excess bran (a) Present (b) Absent	
	Visibly free from insects	(a) Yes (b) No	
	Uniformity in size	(a) Yes (b) No	
	Uniformity in shape	(a) Yes (b) No	
Rice	Foreign matter	Stones/pebbles (a) Present (b) Absent Dirt/Mud (a) Present (b) Absent Excess bran (a) Present (b) Absent	
	Visibly free from insects	(a) Yes (b) No	
	Uniformity in size	(a) Yes (b) No	
	Uniformity in shape	(a) Yes (b) No	
Dal	Foreign matter	Stonco/pobblos (a) Present (b) Absent Dirt/Muda) (a) Present (b) Absent	

(Contd...)

Parameters	Indicators	Findings	Observations
		Excess bran (a) Present (b) Absent	
	Visibly free from insects	(a) Yes (b) No	
	Uniformity in size	(a) Yes (b) No	
	Uniformity in shape	(a) Yes (b) No	
Chilly powder	Characteristic odour	(a) Present (b) Absent	
	Brand	(a) AGMARK certified (b) Non certified	
	Visibly free from insects	(a) Yes (b) No	
Turmeric powder	Characteristic odour	(a) Present (b) Absent	
	Brand	(a) AGMARK certified (b) Non certified	
	Visibly free from insects	(a) Yes (b) No	
Salt	Iodised salt	(a) Present (b) Absent	
	Brand	(a) ISI certified (b) AGMARK (c) Non certified	
Oil	Fortified with vitamin A and D (provided by govt.)	(a) Yes (b) No	
	Brand	(a) ISI certified (b) AGMARK (c) Non certified	

Sample 8: Knowledge attitude practices (kap) of mdm staff towards the mid-day meal programme

Form No. Date

General Information:

Name	
Age	
Sex	
Religion	
Caste	
Appointed as	
Appointed by	
Salary	
No. of family members	

Mid-day Meal Information:

Sr. No.	Questions	Responses
1.	**MDM's OBJECTIVES**	
1.1	Please list some of the objectives of the mid-day meal programme.	(a) Protecting children from classroom hunger (b) Increasing school enrolment and attendance (c) Decreasing the drop-out rate (d) Improving socialization among all the castes (e) Addressing the issue of malnutrition among children (f) Social empowerment of women by creating employment
1.2	Do you think that the mdm has been able to achieve the objectives that you mentioned?	(a) Yes (b) No
2	**PROCUREMENT DETAILS**	
2.1	Are there any problems in procurement of grains and other cooking materials?	(a) Yes (b) No

(Contd…)

Sr. No.	Questions	Responses
2.2	Who maintains the record?	(a) Deputy mamlatdar (b) MDM in charge (c) Cook (d) Teacher (e) Principal
2.3	Are the records cross checked?	(a) Yes (b) No
2.4	In case of shortfall, what is done?	(a) Food served only on some days in a week (b) Quantity of food per child is reduced (c) Food served only until the stock lasts (d) New stock is bought (e) People donate grains (f) Others
2.5	Describe the quality of grains	(a) Excellent (b) Very good (c) Good (d) Average (e) Below average (f) Poor
2.6	Give the list of vegetables that you use.	
2.7	Is there a fixed vendor from whom the vegetables are bought?	(a) Yes (b) No
2.8	Is the purchasing place near by?	(a) Yes (b) No
2.9	Which are the locally available vegetables?	
3	**MONITORING, PERCEPTIONS ON MDMP**	
3.1	Since the beginning of the academic year, has the mid-day meal been inspected?	(a) Yes (b) No
3.2	If yes, then who inspected?	(a) Deputy Collector (b) Deputy Mamlatdar (c) Principal (d) Teacher (e) Others

(Contd…)

Sr. No.	Questions	Responses
3.3	How many times has it been inspected in a month?	(a) Once (b) Twice (c) Thrice
3.4	Are you happy with the salary that you get?	(a) Yes (b) No
3.5	If no, then what are your expectations?	
3.6	What foods would children like to eat which are feasible with the given budget?	
3.7	Mention the problems that you face in running the MDMP successfully.	(a) Inadequate infrastructure (b) Poor finance allocation (c) Shortage of food grains (d) Non co-operation from teachers (e) Low wages (f) Other
3.8	Some positive aspects of MDM that you have felt over a period of time	(a) Children come to school more regularly (b) Social integration (c) Women empowerment (d) Higher retention rates and decreased drop out rates (e) Children getting at least one good meal in a day (f) Other
3.9	Please give your valuable suggestions to improve the programme.	

Sample 9: Knowledge attitude practices (kap) of the teachers towards the mid-day meal programme.

Form No. Date

General Information

1.	School number and address	
2.	Name of the school	
3.	School shift	(a) Morning (b) Afternoon
4.	Medium of education	(a) Gujarati (b) Hindi (c) Other
5.	Name of the Principal/teacher	
6.	Age and sex	
7.	Religion and caste	
8.	Number of teachers in the school	

Information on MDMP

Sr. No.	Questions	Responses
9.	Are cooked meals provided in the school?	(a) Yes (b) No
10.	Are you involved in the MDM programme in anyway?	(a) Yes (b) No
11.	According to you, what are some of the objectives of the MDMP?	(a) Protecting children from classroom hunger (b) Increasing school enrolment and attendance (c) Decreasing the drop-out rate (d) Improving socialization among all the castes (e) Addressing the issue of malnutrition among children (f) Social empowerment of women by creating employment
12.	Do you think that the MDM should continue?	(a) Yes (b) No

(Contd...)

Sr. No.	Questions	Responses
13.	Are you aware of the weekly menu?	(a) Yes (b) No
14.	Give the weekly menu and rate as per the preference of the children. (0-disliked, 1-like, 2-like very much)	

Days	Menu	Degree of Liking		
Monday		0	1	2
Tuesday		0	1	2
Wednesday		0	1	2
Thursday		0	1	2
Friday		0	1	2
Saturday		0	1	2

15.	Do you feel that MDM disrupts classroom process in anyway?	(a) Yes (b) No
16.	How would you rate the interest level of pupils in studies after the MDM?	(a) Highly interested (b) Same as before (c) Not at all interested
17.	Has MDM contributed to social integration?	(a) Yes (b) No
18.	If yes, then how?	
19.	In your perception what are the advantages that the MDM offers?	(a) Universalization of primary education (b) Regular school attendance (c) Improves nutritional and health status of children (d) Improves the social values in children (e) Increases female enrolment (f) Better academic performances (g) Decreased drop-out rates (h) Higher retention rates (i) Improves academic performances (j) Reduces morbidities among children

(Contd...)

20.	In your perception what are some of the drawbacks that hinder with the effective implementation of the programme.	(a) Poor motivation among the staff (b) Low wages for the MDM staff (c) Monotonous and nutritionally inadequate menu (d) Inadequate infrastructure and sanitation (e) Irregular supplies and monitoring (f) Other
21.	Do you think that the food provided by MDMS is nutritious?	(a) Yes (b) No
22.	Should NHE be introduced in the school curriculum?	(a) Yes (b) No
23.	How often do you visit the kitchen while the MDM is being prepared?	(a) Once (b) Twice (c) Other (d) Never
24	Do you think the staffs follows proper hygiene practices during the cooking process?	(a) Yes (b) No
26	Please give your valuable suggestions to improve the programme.	(a) MDM should provide variety in the menu (b) MDM should be given only to the most vulnerable (c) MDM should provide rice based recipes (d) Other

Sample 10: Knowledge attitude practices (kap) of students towards the mid day meal programme

Form No. Date:

Name of the Student:

Name of the School:

Standard:

Years since consuming the MDM:

Sr. No.	Questions	Responses
1.	Do you consume the MDM?	(a) Yes (b) No
2.	How many times in a week do you consume the MDM?	(a) Daily (b) 4-5 times a week (c) 2-3 times a week (d) Once a week (e) Never
3.	Do you like the meal served in the school?	(a) Yes (b) No
4.	Why do you consume the school meal?	(a) Feel hungry (b) Food is tasty (c) Improves health (d) Improves concentration (e) Enjoy eating with others (f) Compulsion (g) Other
5.	Why do not you consume the school meal?	(a) Do not feel hungry (b) Food is not of my liking (c) Food is not tasty (d) Is not a compulsion (e) Bring tiffin from home (f) Fall ill after consuming the MDM (g) Any other
6.	Which menus do you like the most?	(a) Dal bhaat (b) Vaghareli khichdi (c) Dal dhokdl (d) All the recipes (e) Other
7.	Which menu you don't like at all?	(a) Fada khichdi (b) Meethi lapsi (c) Other (d) None

(Contd...)

Sr. No.	Questions	Responses
8.	Which foods would you like to eat in the school?	
9.	Do you get a feeling of satiety after consuming MDM?	(a) Yes (b) No
10.	Where do you consume the MDM?	(a) School (b) Home
11.	If at home, do you share it with anyone?	(a) Yes (b) No
12.	Do you think that the MDM should continue?	(a) Yes (b) No
13.	Mention some positive aspects of MDM that you have felt over a period of time.	(a) Weight has increased (b) Height has increased (c) Fall ill less often (d) Concentration power has increased (e) Feel energetic (f) Better academic scores (g) More regular in school (h) All friends sit together and eat (i) Other
14.	Mention some drawbacks of the MDM	(a) Hinders with quality learning (b) The quantity of food provided is not sufficient (c) Poor quality of food (d) Other
15.	What suggestions can you give to improve the MDMP	(a) Increase the quantity of food (b) Improve the quality of food (c) Should not affect the teaching time (d) Include some variety foods (e) Seasonal fruits should be given (f) Other

5 Public Private Partnership
Akshaypatra

This chapter deals with initiation of a public private partnership – Akshay Patra which aims to provide a nutritious school meal to the underpriviledged children of India.

Akshay Patra has been initiated since June 2000 in Bangalore with the vision that "*No child in India shall be deprived of education because of hunger.*" The earliest efforts covered 1500 children in 5 schools, when there was no State run school meal programme in Karnataka. These initiatives received over whelming response which gave an impetus to the growth of "The AkshayaPatra Foundation".

The Supreme Court of India passed an order in November 28, 2001 which mandated that: "Cooked mid-day meal is to be provided in all the government and government-aided primary schools in all the states."

Akshaya Patra was called in to give testimonies to the Supreme Court in order to implement the mandate and received the support of the Ministry of Human Resource Development (Department of School Health and Education) in 2003, when the foundation was already reaching out to 23,000 underprivileged children through the support of various donors. Today "The Akshaya Patra Foundation" has grown from a small endeavor to a mammoth force, with the partnership of the Government of India & various State governments, as well as the generosity of thousands of supporters and reaches out to 1.2 million children everyday.

PROGRAMME IMPLEMENTATION

1. The guidelines issued by the Central Government are considered by the State Governments while implementing the scheme.
2. A National Steering-cum-Monitoring Committee set up at the national level monitors the programme, assesses the impact and provides policy advice to Central and State Governments.
3. Central assistance in the form of subsidies is released upon submission of the committee's Annual Work Plan by the Programme Approval Board.
4. A nodal department is authorized to take responsibility and implementation cells are organised by the nodal department and one officer is appointed at each district and block level to oversee effective implementation of the programme.
5. The Panchayats/Urban Local Bodies are in charge of the scheme in states where primary education is entrusted to them.
6. The Ministry of Human Resource Development is the nodal agency for sanctioning of funds and supply of food grains (central assistance) to the states on behalf of the Government of India.
7. The foundation has to set up kitchen, carry out the day to day operations of preparing meals and maintain its running costs as the NP-NSPE, 2006 Guidelines state. 'In urban areas where a centralized kitchen setup is possible for a cluster of schools, cooking is undertaken in a centralized kitchen and cooked hot meal is then transported under hygienic conditions through a reliable transport system to various schools. There may be one or more such nodal kitchen(s) in an urban area, depending on the number of clusters which they serve.
8. Other expenses such as cooks honorarium, vessels and kitchen construction, transportation is to be borne by

NGO. Thought the Government makes provisions for raising donations based on the results of the evaluations undertaken.

9. A National level Steering-cum-Monitoring Committee (NSMC) oversees management and monitoring of the programme. As stated in NP-NPSE, 2006.

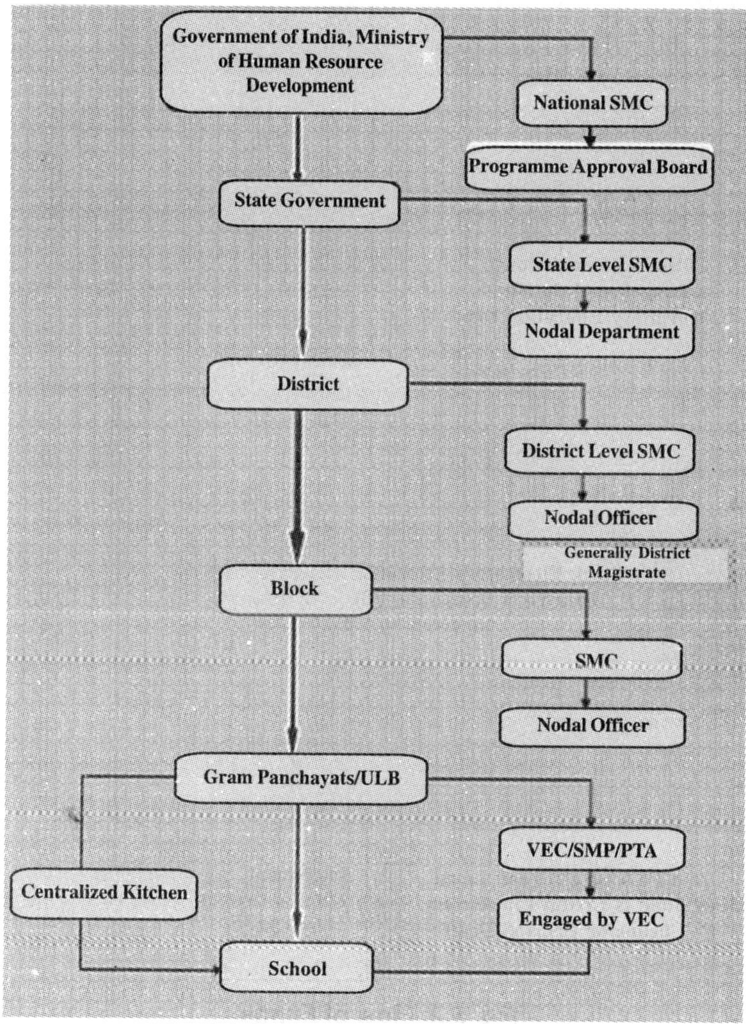

Fig. 5.1: Programme Implementation

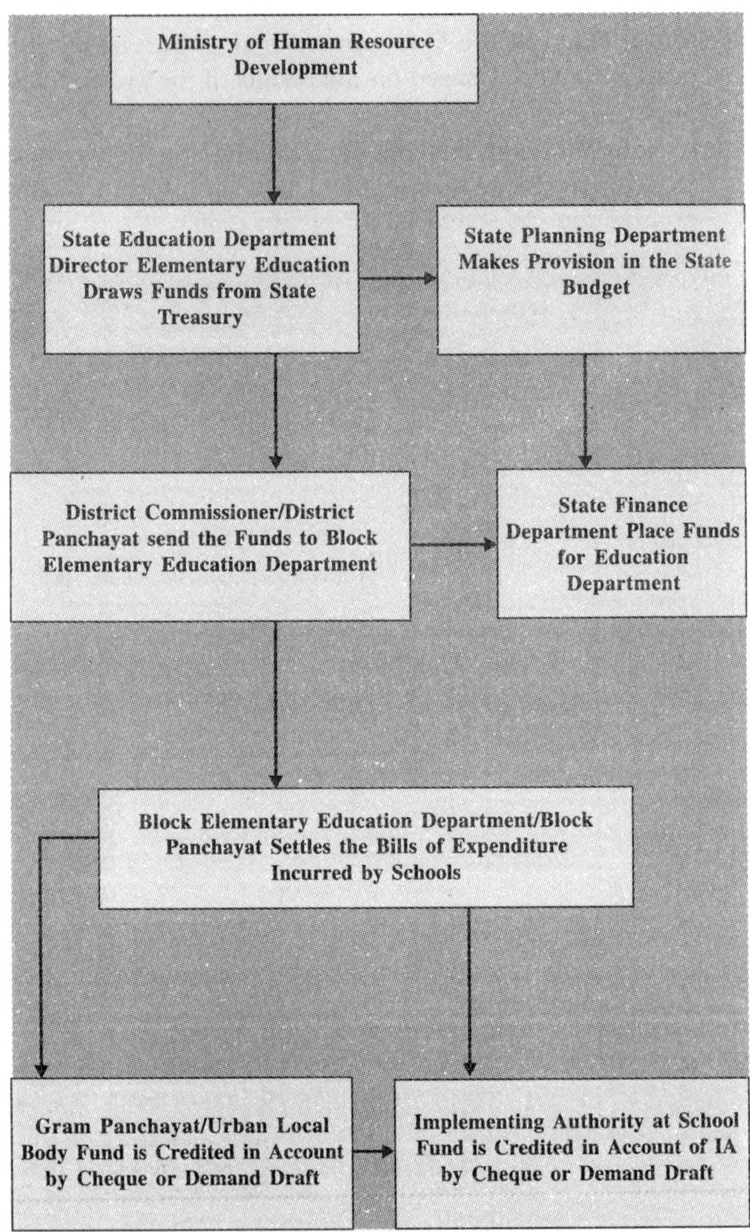

Fig. 5.2: Flow of Funds

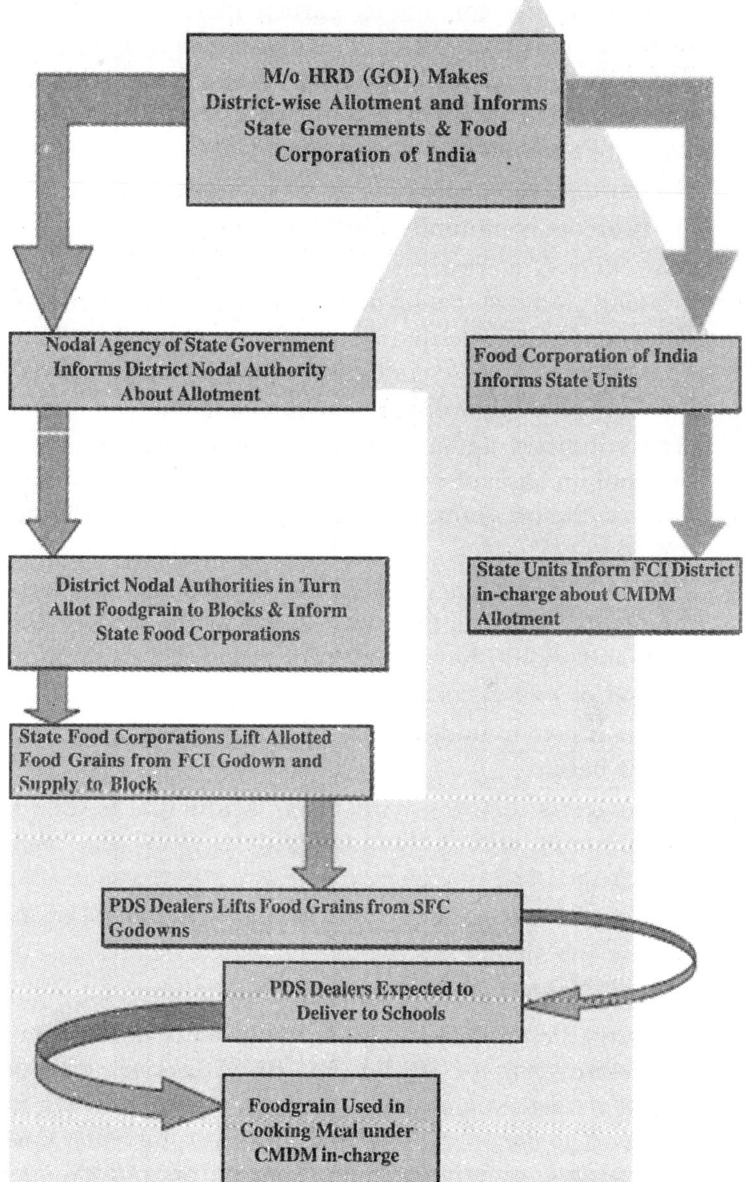

Fig. 5.3: Flow of Grains

AKSHAY PATRA'S ROLE OF NGO

NGO promotes community participation through active volunteering and fundraising. It involves all layers of society and helps the Government make the mid-day meal scheme a 'peoples programme'. There is a two-pronged strategy to the Government's decision to encourage NGOs:

1. To improve the quality of the programme
2. To promote community involvement.

The State Government considers many facets before undertaking partnership with non-profitable Non Government Organisation (NGO) such as Akshaya Patra. Apart from being transparent and 'of proven integrity', following other criteria's as stated by NP-NSPE, 2006 should be fulfilled.

- The voluntary agency should not discriminate in any manner on basis of religion, caste and creed, and should not use the programme for propagation of any religious practice.
- The voluntary agency should be a body that is registered under the Societies Registration Act or the Public Trust Act, and should have been in existence for a minimum period of two years.
- Commitment to undertake supply responsibility on a no-profit basis.
- Willingness to work with PRIs/ Municipal bodies in accordance with relevant guidelines of the State Government
- Financial and logistic capacity to supply the MDM on the requisite scale

OUTREACH AND ACHIEVEMENTS

- Akshaya Patra works in partnership with various State Governments of India to provide 1.2 million underprivileged children across the nation with school lunch. It is the world's largest NGO run mid-day meal programme, present in 18 locations of the country.

- Food lab of Akshaya Patra strives to ensure that the meals are palatable to children, while also meeting the requirements of a growing child. The Foundation's centralized kitchens, some of the largest in the world, use innovative technology to cook hundreds of thousands of meals in a few short hours. While the decentralized kitchens reach out to children in the remotest areas of India while also creating employment for hundreds of women.
- In some areas where Akshaya Patra is providing meals, enrolment for class 1 students has increased by as much as 41 per cent during the initial year of implementation.
- The Karnataka Human Development Report 2005 explains, the Government of Karnataka was the 'first to take this step' of involving NGOs in development programmes.
- This pioneering move, by the Government of Karnataka, to make NGOs the implementing arm of the Government has been one of the major reasons for its success in attaining the goals of the programme.
- By setting up and encouraging private-public partnerships, the government is successfully leveraging the skills and resources of the private sector for the greater good. Today, India's mid-day meal scheme is one of the largest school lunch programmes in the world, reaching out to nearly 120 million children in the country.
- Each centralized kitchen has the capacity to cook between 50 000 to 150 000 meals daily thus achieving economies of scale. Cooking takes place in mechanized, steam heated cauldrons custom built to reduce the cook to consume time.
- Mechanization has helped to meet the highest standards of hygiene by minimizing human handling of food. Freshly cooked food is packed in stainless steel containers and transported to various schools in custom built vehicles (about 10 to 15 schools per vehicle). Security personnel

escort each vehicle to ensure safe delivery of meals. There are two types of menus prepared throughout the country: North Indian and South Indian. The North Indian menu consists of three items: roti, sabji and rice while the South Indian menu also consists of rice, sambar and curd.

- Decentralized kitchens are set up in remote areas of the country where difficult terrain makes setting up of large infrastructures infeasible. Self-help groups (in many cases women's groups) are identified, who will then carry out the cooking process. They are trained and educated to prepare the meals in a healthy, hygienic manner and provided with all the raw materials and infrastructure required for cooking.
- The Akshaya Patra representatives are responsible for the operations and smooth running of the programme. We monitor the entire process to ensure that the children get the best meals.
- Feedback is taken from the school authorities, parents and, most importantly the children, to maintain the high quality that has become the hallmark of our programme.
- A unique feature of this model is that quite often, the women cooking the meals are the mothers of the children we reach out to. Hundreds of such mothers have benefitted from the programme. Not only do they get to cook food for their own sons and daughters, but also gain a certain amount of financial independence from the employment created.
- Table 5.1 given below gives details on the area, total number of students covered type of kitchen under the AkshayaPatra Foundation.

Table 5.1
Details on the Coverage of Akshaya Patra

State/Location	Number of Children	Number of Schools	Type of Kitchen
Andhra Pradesh	**42,544**	**247**	
Vishakhapatnam	5,410	7	Centralized Kitchen
Hyderabad	37,134	240	Centralized Kitchen
Assam	**36,664**	**386**	
Guwahati	36,664	386	Centralized Kitchen
Chhattisgarh	31,757	156	
Bhilai	31,757	156	Centralized Kitchen
Gujarat	**256,008**	**971**	
Ahmedabad	129,224	524	Centralized Kitchen
Vododara	126,784	447	Centralized Kitchen
Karnataka	**537,671**	**2,439**	
Bangalore	101,482	387	Centralized Kitchen
Bellary	120,858	574	Centralized Kitchen
Hubli	176,344	778	Centralized Kitchen
Mangalore	20,286	115	Centralized Kitchen
Mysore	15,058	56	Centralized Kitchen
Vasanthapura	103,643	529	Centralized Kitchen
Orissa	**63,841**	**623**	
Puri	49,078	441	Centralized Kitchen
Nayagarh	14,763	182	Decentralized Kitchen
Rajasthan	**159,763**	**1,745**	
Jaipur	131,240	1,397	Centralized Kitchen
Nathdwara	14,759	176	Centralized Kitchen
Baran	13,764	172	Decentralized Kitchen
Uttar Pradesh	**169,801**	**1,629**	
Vrindavan	169,801	1,629	Decentralized Kitchen
Total	1,298,049	8,196	

6 Future Ahead

DEVELOPING COLLABORATION AND ADOPTING AN INTEGRATED APPROACH

The Government of India (2008) document suggests an adoption of effective collaborations at all levels for successful implementation of any welfare programmes. The NPNSPE guidelines (2006) suggest an involvement of local bodies and community. Linkages with other developmental programmes such as ICDS, Sampoorna Grameen Rozgar Yojana and Prime Minister's Grameen Yojana could be used for creating physical facilities like improvement in infrastructural support at school level including staffing and financial parameters with due regard to effectiveness, sustainability and replicability.

HEALTH SYSTEM RESEARCH

Health Systems Research (HSR) is a field of inquiry examining the organisation, financing, performance, and impact of health systems – defined as the constellation of governmental and non-governmental actors that influence population health, including health care providers, insurers, purchasers, public health agencies, community-based organisations, and entities that operate outside the traditional sphere of health care (National Library of Medicines, 2007). The International Development Research Center in its module states that the HSR has proved to be a useful tool for health decision makers at all levels over the past 20 years, providing them with the necessary data for informed decision making.

Applying HSR helps in creating foundation for evidence-informed policymaking, especially when resources are limited. It allows for the effective combination of research and policy (Corlien et al, 2003).

The HSR approach can be used to identify the related departments and address interrelated problems in any developmental programme from the differing perspectives of all those who are, directly or indirectly, involved for enhancing the efficiency and effectiveness of the programmes with full involvement of all partners. Thus Health System Research can be applied as a strategy to achieve Intersectoral collaboration as an essential element for a large scale multidimensional programme like MDM. Departmental study (Nambiar and Gandhi, 2008) have shown effective use of HSR in augmenting the MDM with green leafy vegetables.

RAPID APPRAISAL SURVEY

The Rapid Appraisal Survey (RAS) methods consist of combination of various qualitative and quantitative methodologies of gathering information. The RAS enables local people and outsiders to plan together appropriate interventions and evaluate the impact of development interventions after these have been carried out (Bergeron, 1999).

Development workers consider the RAS tools appropriate for gathering information at the beginning of an intervention, as part of a process of appraisal and planning. However, RAS tools have a much wider range of potential uses (Alur, Nath and Kumar, 2005).

BEHAVIOUR CHANGE COMMUNICATION

Behaviour Change Approaches (BCC)have been widely used to increase the impact of Health and Nutrition programmes. The principle behind Behaviour Change Approaches is that in order to successfully change behaviours, programmes must reduce barriersto change as well as convince stakeholders of the benefits of change (Tholakele and Mpumalanga, 2003).

Inbuilt BCC strategy in MDM is essential to acquaint the grass-root level participants with the NP-NSPE guidelines and increases their liable partaking, thus aiding in success of a mammoth programme like MDM (Bakshi and Sharma, 2008). Effective BCC using posters have shown easier understanding and early adaptation of changed behaviour among the MDM staff (Nambiar and Gandhi, 2008).Applying effective BCC strategies by using different communication channels such as posters, guidelines, lectures, and workshops can help create awareness and sensitize the teaching staff towards MDMP (Sharma et al, 2006).

Safety education programme, have reported improved practices among food handlers such as hand washing, maintaining safe food temperatures, preventing cross contamination, and pest management more frequently, compared to before the programme (Anding et at, 2007). In a school feeding programme, it is essential to ensure hygienic quality of meal. The cooks should be trained to observe strict personal hygiene and hygienic handling of foods during each stem right from procurement to distribution (NFI, 2003).

CAPACITY BUILDING

Capacity building is defined as the "process of developing and strengthening the skills, instincts, abilities, processes and resources that organisations and communities need to survive, adapt, and thrive in the fast-changing world." (Philbin,1996).

Under a study carried in the government sector of Philippine, the approach of capacity building has proved to be helpful for governments in identifying priority families and communities for intervention, as well as rationalize the allocation of its social development funds. More importantly, it helped in making definite steps to encourage community participation in situation analysis, planning, monitoring and evaluation of social development projects by building the capacity of local government officials, indigenous leaders and other stakeholders to converge in the management of these concerns.

Capacity building is also a key strategy to improve food safety in developing countries. Many officials and workers were trained in the HACCP approach using capacity building. Moreover improving and extending the benefits of school nutrition programme, in terms of improved dietary habits, school based gardening, and etc can be strengthened by applying capacity building at various levels in the system (FAO, 2004).

PARTICIPATORY MONITORING AND EVALUATION

The NP-NSPE, 2006 guidelines suggests on establishing a monitoring system at every level for effective implementation of the MDMP. Under this condition Participatory monitoring can be the best strategy. Participatory monitoring (PM) allows the people working together to learn, solve problems, and refine programmes by gathering and using information. It aims to make monitoring a useful process for all decision makers, researchers as well as grass-root level workers. PM helps decision makers, at every level to define and measure success in their own terms by providing information about programme progress that is accessible and meaningful. Participatory techniques enhance qualitative methodologies by creating an interactive relationship with decision makers that fosters dialogue. PM allows involving beneficiaries, staff from nongovernmental and community-based organisations (NGOs and CBOs), and health care providers.

Apart the degree of participation affects the outcome for any project:

1. Information dissemination: one-way flow of information.
2. Dialogue: two-way exchange of information.
3. Collaboration: shared control over decision-making
4. Empowerment: transfer of resources and decision-making.

A strong monitoring and information systems should essentially be established in a huge programme like the MDMS to evaluate the progress at regular intervals. Emphasis on the community or government actions for a scheme like the mid-day meal is equally essential (Khera, 2006).

DIVERSE INTERVENTIONS UNDER MDMP

A number of interventions are likely to promote the health and nutritional status of our school children. Health and nutrition education, sanitation and hygiene programmes, school gardening projects, environmental projects, health check-up projects and many more. Developing effective synergies with various local departments and other welfare programmes can help to overcome the assorted issues that affect the quality of services under the mid-day meal scheme.

School health and nutrition programmes have become an increasingly common component of the education sector response to "Education for All."

Schools offer a readily available platform where teachers as a skilled work force in closed contact with the community can work together for holistic development of children; with a strong support and involvement of various developmental schemes and programmes that possibly affect the school feeding programme (FAO, 2004).

There is a growing awareness of the link between children's nutritional and health status, and their educational participation and performance. Thus school feeding should be made a part of a larger school nutrition and health programme.

MDM is a platform for strengthening the school health programme. The school health service system should consist of more than routine medical checkup. It must strive to ensure healthy environment in schools, environmental sanitation and provision of safe drinking water. School meal programme when combined with deworming of children, vitamin A supplementation and iron and folic acid supplementation, it yields good results (NFI, 2003). The benefit of school meal programme will be vastly improved if it is ensured that school health service is in its place in the same schools, which would help in making the programme holistic.

SCHOOL KITCHEN GARDEN

Nutritionally inadequate diet, monotonous menus, lack of fresh fruits and vegetables are the common issues in the mid-day meal programme. It is important that the mid-day meal should contain good quantity of vegetables particularly, dark GLV'S as these are important to combat micronutrient deficiencies. Hence, efforts should be made to encourage school gardens where there is adequate space (NFI, 2003).

India with subtropical climate has no predicament in growing vegetables. Yet consumption has remained low in the earlier decades; due to low production, poor access and affordability. This alarming situation has also reflected over the mid-day meals that hinders in the objective of supplementing a micro-nutrient rich diet, hence exhibiting its inefficiency in combating nutritional deficiencies.

International agencies like the UNICEF and FAO have helped to initiate school gardening projects in India. School kitchen gardens in Pune, Karnataka, Delhi have shown positive achievements. Students have benefited by improved academic performance, increase in confidence level, their learning interest has increased. Moreover, children have developed increased liking for fruits and vegetables (FAO, 2004).

Partnerships can lead to sustainable programmes and an integrated approach provides one of the ideal and rare opportunities for the governments to collaborate. Moreover different departments learn about each other's systems, thereby contributing in sustainable effects.

POSITIVE DEVIANCE-A NOVEL APPROACH FOR MDM IN SCHOOLS OF URBAN VADODARA

Positive deviance (PD) is an asset based approach that "seeks to identify and optimize existing Resources and solutions within the community to solve community problems.

Moreover using a positive deviance approach in community development programmes has shown success in achieving the objectives (Sternin et al, 1998). Applying a P.D approach in MDM can enable the programme staff and their community partners identify the unique practices of some community members, thereby improving in current practices within the same environment. This approach can successfully be used to handle minor managerial issues related to MDM (Levinson et al, 2004). The PD Approach has been used successfully to design nutrition programmes since the 1980s. In the context of education, positive deviant have shown to improve the enrolment rate, especially for girls.

Given below is a case study of Positive Deviance for MDMP in schools of urban Vadodara.

Positive and Negative Deviant Behaviours Affecting the Mid Day Meal Programme (MDMP) in Government Aided Primary Schools of an Urban Indian City: Causes, Consequences and Solutions

The condition of Indian children is best described as a permanent humanitarian emergency though the GOI has spent more than Rs 9550 crores on the Mid Day Meal Programme (MDMP). MDMP evaluations across the country have revealed both success stories as well as critical issues related to its implementation. Some reports testify that MDM increases attendance, improves quality of education, brings social and gender equity. However various drawbacks listed vary from lack of information on the NP-NSPE guidelines; inadequate funds for utensils and infrastructure, low and delayed reimbursement of salaries; lack of support from school staff and poor working conditions which lead to low motivation in the MDM staff members. Reports also reveal no usage of vegetables in MDM, unhygienic cooking and working conditions, lack of variety in the menu and interrupted services with compromised quality. Meagre resource availability, lack of awareness and no decision making power slays the enthusiasm of service providers at grass root levels; which further leads to poor output of the project. These conditions need to be improved using innovative and sustainable approaches such as *positive deviance approach,* especially when the budget earmarked for year 2010-11 was Rs. 9440 crores.

Innovative strategies such as Positive Deviance Approach (PDA) have been successfully used for bringing about positive changes in the psychosocial and behavioural considerations among the communities as well as health workers. PDA has a potential to learn from the existing community situations and reduce poverty and improve social inclusion in the public sector. PDA has been used worldwide to combat such intractable problems as childhood malnutrition, sex trafficking of girls and poor infant health. The MDMP involves barriers with respect to the logistics management and political interests, therefore use of PDA in a resource constrained setting PDA could be a sustainable approach. Considering the effectiveness of PDA, it could be used as a strategy to bring desirable behaviour changes among the grass root level service providers and beneficiaries. Moreover, no reports on the use of PDA for improvement of MDM scheme are available; hence the present study was planned with following objectives:

1. To identify positive and negative deviant practices followed by MDM staff members, teachers and students.
2. To apply PDA for bringing desirable behavioural changes for improving services provided under MDM.

Methods

Multistage Systematic Random sampling technique was applied to select 7/121 Government aided schools of urban Vadodara. MDM staff members (n = 29), school teachers (n= 35) and students consuming MDM (n= 1333) were enrolled in the study.

Rapid Appraisal Survey (RAS), a qualitative research methodology that enables to obtain quick information from the local population about their conditions and needs, was used to elicit data. Areas under the survey were:

1. Food handling practices (cooking and serving).
2. Adherence to and nutritional quality of cyclic MDM menu.
3. Sanitation and hygiene practices followed by the MDM staff members, students and teachers.

4. Monitoring and evaluation by the teachers and MDM authorities.

Under each major head, 5 ideal practices as mentioned in the NP-NSPE guidelines were observed and listed, and these were given a total score point of "10" (2 points to every ideal practice). School that scored more than "6" points in each major head was recognized as a PD school and practices followed were used to design a PDA for rest of the 6 schools.

Designing and disseminating the Positive Deviance Approach in 6 schools:

A traditional Positive Deviant Approach with 6 steps: "6- approach" was followed in the study.

1. *Defining the problem and desired outcome:* Based on findings of RAS; difficulty in quality implementation of the MDM programme was identified as the problem and the desired outcome was to improve the quality of programme implementation in available resources.
2. *Determine the presence of PD individuals:* Factors influencing PD practices and characteristics required in the change agent were categorized. Discussions were conducted with all the grass root level service providers (teaching staff and MDM staff members) to orient them on PDA followed by electing the principal and the MDM supervisor as a change agent.
3. *Discover uncommon but successful behaviours and strategies through an inquiry:* Key informants interviews and participatory observations were undertaken to identify the uncommon practices, behaviours and techniques followed by PD individuals in the positive deviant school during/under difficult situations.
4. *Develop or Design initiative based on the inquiry findings:* Posters using realistic photographs from the PD school were made for teachers, MDM staff members and students for bringing behavioural change in sanitation and hygiene, food handling practices and nutrition and health importance of MDM, cyclic menu and ration usage

ready reckoner. Training sessions for the change agents and participatory monitoring and evaluations were undertaken.

5. *Discern the effectiveness of the initiative:* Followed by designing and implementation of the PDA, a feedback was taken from the target groups and the initiatives of positive deviant approach were continued for a period of 2 months.
6. *Disseminate the successful initiative:* Assuring the acceptance of the PD initiatives, 10 posters with tailor made messages were developed. The key messages for the MDM staff included the cyclic menu, serving amount and macronutrients available from that amount, amount of ration usage per batch of 100-200 children as per the menu and general food handling practices. The posters for teachers included importance of monitoring and cleanliness. While messages for children focused on the health and nutritional importance of MDM and general cleanliness. The posters were explained to the teachers and students during assemblies and before serving of MDM, while the MDM staff was personally counseled twice a week by the investigator.

After the intervention of two months, change in practices of MDM staff members, teachers and students towards the ideal practices listed under each major head were evaluated using RAS. In order to compute the qualitative improvement, changes were recorded as scores and expressed as percentages to compare changes between the schools pre and post intervention period.

Results

Baseline Data

Rapid Appraisal Survey was undertaken to amass baseline data from 7 selected schools. On basis of the NP-NSPE guidelines, 4 major areas with 5 ideal practices under each were evaluated and given *Ideal Practice Scores*. As shown in Table 6.1, school Number IV scored maximum points, 8/10

Table 6.1

Identifying PD Practices as Compared with the NP-NSPE Guidelines Based on the Developed Scores

Sr. No.	Parameters	School Code Numbers						
		I	II	III	IV	V	VI	VII
	Food Handling Practices							
1.	Store room available	√	√	X	√	X	√	√
2.	Separate kitchen shade available	√	√	√	√	√	√	√
3.	Safe food storage facility	X	§	§§	√	§§	X	§
4.	Adequate utensils (storing, cooking and serving)	√	X	√	√	X	X	X
5.	Platforms in the kitchen	X	X	X	X	X	X	X
	Scores	6/10	5/10	4/10	8/10	2/10	4/10	5/10
	Adherence to and Nutritional Quality of MDM							
1.	Display of cyclic menu	X	X	X	√	X	X	X
2.	Daily usage of vegetables	X	X	X	√	X	X	X
3.	Adherence to the cyclic menu	X	X	X	√	X	X	X
4.	Proportionate ration usage	§	X	§	√	X	§	X
5.	Gas line connection/LPG bottles	√	√	√	√	√	√	√
	Scores	3/10	2/10	3/10	10/10	2/10	3/10	2/10

(Contd…)

Sr. No.	Parameters	School Code Numbers						
		I	II	III	IV	V	VI	VII
	Sanitation and Hygiene Practices							
1.	Separate serving area available	§	§	X	√	X	X	X
2.	Personal sanitation by MDM staff	X	√	§	√	√	√	√
3.	Left over thrown disposed in VMC vans	X	X	X	√	√	X	X
4.	Water available for entire day	§	√	√	√	√	√	√
5.	Closed drainage	√	√	√	√	§	√	√
	Scores	4/10	7/10	5/10	10/10	7/10	6/10	6/10
	Monitoring and Supervision							
1.	Presence of principal while serving of MDM	§	X	§	√	X	√	§
2.	Presence of at least 2 teachers while serving of MDM	X	X	§	√	X	X	X
3.	Quality assurance of cooked MDM	§	§	√	√	X	X	√
4.	Presence of In charge during ration usage	X	X	√	√	§	§	X
5.	Supervision of cleanliness during serving and consumption of MDM	X	§	§	√	√	X	§
	Scores	2/10	2/10	7/10	10/10	3/10	3/10	4/10

* School with highlight is a PD school, Numeric in parenthesis is the score amount √ - Present (2) § - Partially present (1) X – Absent (0) §§- Not applicable (0)

in Food Handling Practices and 10/10 Adherence to and Nutritional Quality of MDM, Sanitation and hygiene practices and Monitoring and evaluation by the teachers and MDM authorities. School number IV was thus identified as the *Positive deviant School.* Further observations were made to enlist the uncommon, unique and positive practices in the PD school (Table 6.2), these are listed below. Figure 6.1 describes the parameters that affected the positive and negative behaviours of the individuals.

(a) Allocation of an extra class as a store room by the school authorities, which was kept very clean.
(b) Storage of raw ration on benches or on shelves properly covered to avoid any direct infestation/contamination.
(c) Display of the cyclic menu outside the MDM kitchen under supervision of the MDM supervisor.
(d) Use of greens as well as seasonal vegetables everyday in MDM.
(e) Correct usage of ration per child for cooking (cooked food vs actual beneficiaries).
(f) Clean cooking and serving area.
(g) Regular monitoring of serving of MDM by school teachers.
(h) Hand washing before eating food.

While in the non PD schools, the ration and spices were kept on the floor, though the store room was clean, there was no ventilation, it was dark and dingy and pests such as rodents, flies, cockroaches and ants were found in 57.14 per cent schools. The spices and utensils were kept uncovered 42.85 per cent schools. In 42.85 per cent schools only potatoes and brinjal were used as vegetables and less rice, dal, wheat and oil were used as compared to the guidelines in 42.85 per cent schools. In 28.14 per cent schools, cleaning of raw food stuff, serving area and the utensils was not followed properly due to water scarcity. Seventy-five per cent teachers were unaware of the cyclic menu as it was hardly followed. Presence of principal and teachers was not seen while the MDM was being served in 42 per cent of schools.

Table 6.2

Positive Practices Observed in the PD school

Positive Practices in the PD School	Negative Practices in the non PD School with percentage distribution	
Food handling practices (storage, cooking and serving)		
Using desks from schools to keep the gunny bags	Keeping the gunny bags in dark, dingy places on floor	42.85%
Keeping the spices in air tight and separate containers	Keeping the spices in the plastic containers as such on the rack	57.14%
Thoroughly cleaning the vegetables and grains before using	Keeping utensils un covered on the floor	42.85%
Thoroughly washing grains and vegetables at least twice and cleaning the serving area	Not cleaning/washing the grains or vegetables before use nor the serving area	14.28%
Adherence to and quality of cyclic menu		
Displaying the cyclic menu in kitchen	No awareness about the cyclic menu among both teachers and MDM staff members	71.42%
Regular use of different vegetables in available budget	Poor usage (2-3 times a week) of vegetables used, especially GLV	57.14%
Generous use of oil and spices to make food palatable and use of allocated ration	Meager amount of oil and only chilly and turmeric was used in spices. Less amount of ration usage as per the number of children	28.57%

(Contd…)

Positive Practices in the PD School	Negative Practices in the non PD School with percentage distribution	
Properly cooked meal	Presence of stones, insects and foreign materials in cooked food	14.28%
Quality testing of the prepared food by the MDM staff members	No testing of food done by any of the staff members	57.14%
Sanitation and hygiene practices followed by the MDM staff members, students and teachers		
Hands washed by children prior to eating MDM	Disposing the raw and cooked waste in or outside school premises	57.14%
Waste disposed systematically in dustbins by both children and the MDM staff members	No hand washing by children before consuming MDM	42.85%
Different set of clothes worn by the MDM staff members while cooking	Throwing the left over on the open ground of the school	42.85%
Inculcating discipline practices and mannerism among children while consuming MDM	Consuming tobacco while handling food	14.28%
Removing footwear while eating and sitting on mats provided by school	Use of footwear by the MDM staff members while cooking	28.57%

(Contd…)

Positive Practices in the PD School	Negative Practices in the non PD School with percentage distribution	
Monitoring and evaluation		
Presence of principal and 3-4 teachers while serving of MDM	No presence of teaches or principal during implementation of the MDM	85.71%
Monitoring amount of ration used in preparing a day's menu as per the number of children	No check on ration usage and chances of excess or reduced amount of food preparation	57.14%
Motivation by the teachers for participating in MDM and monitoring discipline and cleanliness	No motivation by teachers and no monitoring as well	57.14%

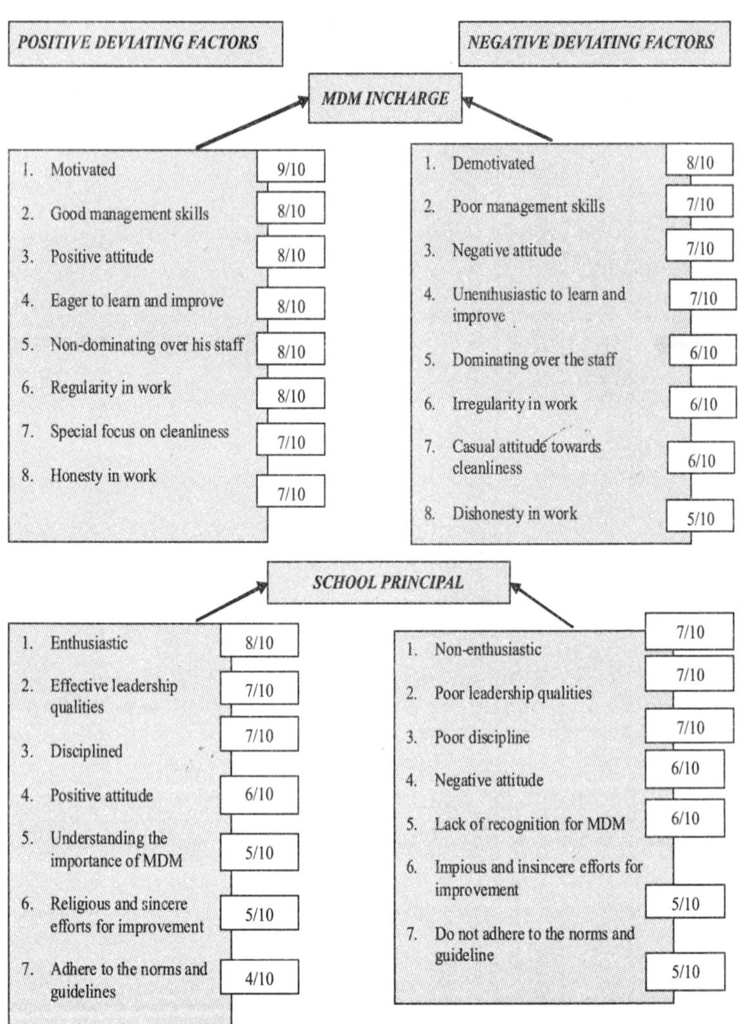

Fig. 6.1: Factors influencing the positive deviance in Sayajigunj school No.1 and factors influencing negative deviance in rest of the 6 schools

* These factors were given score points based on 5 surprise visits. Every factor carried score point 2 thus making a total score of 10. The maximally scored points were marked as positive deviant factors. Based on these the change agents were also identified

Implementation of the Action Plan

Figure 6.2 shows the action plan that was formulated as per the "6D Approach". Uncommon practices were identified in 6 non-PD schools and teachers and MDM staffs were identified as change agents. Using realistic photographs of the PD school, 10 set of posters were made to bring behavioural changes (Poster 1 to 10). For the initial week of intervention period the posters were explained regularly. They were then displayed in the school for reinforcement of the messages. Simultaneously 4 training sessions were conducted with the change agents to assure continuous participatory monitoring.

Impact Assessment

The post data after 2 months revealed that in the PDA, the behaviour change communication strategy, training sessions and participatory activities allowed the subjects to contribute and they also got an opportunity to participate in improving their programme – thus making them feel an important part of the project. They felt motivated and also reported that within the available resources, if the PD school could serve MDM so close to the NP_NSPE guidelines, they can also try to do so.

Under the *food handling practices section (cooking and serving),* 57.14 per cent improvement was seen in storage of raw ingredients and ration and 42.85 per cent school showed improved utensil storage practice. Under *adherence to and nutritional quality of cyclic MDM menu:* 85.71 per cent schools started following the cyclic menu while 71.42 per cent and 57.14 per cent schools increased vegetable and ration usage respectively. The third section of *sanitation and hygiene practices*: 57.14 per cent schools children started washing hands before consuming MDM, removed their shoes while eating MDM. Finally under *monitoring and evaluation by the school staff:* 28.57 per cent teachers started regular monitoring of MDM along with imparting nutrition and health education and extended complete support to the MDM staff members.

A → Problem Identification	B → PD Individuals	C → Major PD Practices	D → Design Initiatives	E → Discern Effectiveness	F Disseminate Initiatives
• Lack of support from the school staff in 85.71% schools • Poor infrastructure & resources in 71.42% schools • Poor understanding about MDM among school and MDM staff members in 71.42% schools	• School principal • MDM in charge • This was uniform in all the seven schools and it was done on basis of the Ideal Practice Scores	• Co-ordination among school and MDM staff • Positive attitude and efficient use of resources • Adhering to MDM guidelines • This was observed in the PD school	• Posters on PD practices separately made for students, teachers and MDM staff members • Training on participatory monitoring (4 sessions with each school)	• Feedbacks were taken for the designed posters, and training sessions from the volunteers to check effectiveness	• Change agents were trained by 4 sessions in each school • Regular posters were displayed during preparation, serving and consumption of MDM in all the schools as a BCC strategy • Participatory monitoring was undertaken by the change agents on regular basis to measure the change

Fig. 6.2: Sequence of Steps and NHE Material Used

Discussion

A public welfare programme like MDM, addresses multiple issues such as education, poverty, gender equality, health and nutrition among children. However, the condition of Indian children is best described as a permanent humanitarian emergency though the GOI has spent Rs 8300 crores (2009-10) and plans to spend more than Rs. 9550 crores in coming years on the Mid Day meal programme and lack of resources, poor MDM quality and quantity, poor infrastructure and support from education department (school principal and teachers) is the common finding reported by several investigators. Divergence in attitudes, low motivation, poor wages and inefficient knowledge of the guidelines among the grass-root level functionaries are also reported.

The campaign for universal, nutritious midday meals in primary schools is rapidly becoming a broad-based "people's movement". Positive deviance has shown a significant improvement in hand hygiene, which was associated with a decrease in the overall incidence of infections in an institutional setting. Whereas similar PDA was used to develop menu guides to reduce cancer risk at household level. Also in an organisational setting, PDA has been successfully used. At community level PDA has been extensively used to alter the infant feeding practices among the mothers and information generated from such studies can be valuable asset in ICDS to empower women.

Since monitoring and evaluations are mandatory as per the NP-NSPE guidelines and Forty One Institutions of Social Science Research, identified for monitoring the Sarva Shiksha Abhiyan, are also entrusted with the task of monitoring the Mid Day Scheme. The Department of Science &Technology (DS & T) has been entrusted the Thrust Area item TA24 on *'Firming up Science & Technology Application in Mid Day Meal'* by the Prime Minister's Office. The overall objective under the identified Thrust Area is to develop appropriate technologies and operational models that will improve the administration of Mid Day Meal Scheme i.e. ensure delivery of warm healthy meals to target groups without incurring high cost.

Table 6.3

Changes Observed in Practices of the Grassroot Level Functionaries

Broad Areas	Parameters	Before Intervention	Actions Observed After Intervention
MDM staff	Non-adherence to the cyclic menu	85.71%	85.71% change
	Limited quantity and variety of vegetables used	71.42%	71.42% improved
	Allocated ration usage	85.71%	57.14% increased
	Open and unhygienic storage of spices and vegetables	85.71%	57.14% improved
	Uncovered storage of utensils	85.71%	42.85% improved
	Improper storing techniques of food grains	71.42%	71.42% change
Teachers	Unaware of cyclic menu	85.71%	28.57% improved
	Lack of monitoring on MDM implementation	85.71%	57.14% change
	Lack of support and co-ordination with MDM staff	85.71%	28.57% change
	Poor record keeping and manipulation of data	85.71%	42.85% improved
	No education on nutrition, health and sanitation given to children	85.71%	28.57% change
Students	No hand washing	85.71%	57.14% change
	Not removing shoes while eating	85.71%	
	Poor vegetable consumption	85.71%	
	Disposing the leftover food in school premises	85.71%	42.85% change
	Wastage of food	85.71%	
	Unaware of importance of MDM	85.71%	

Poster 1 to 4

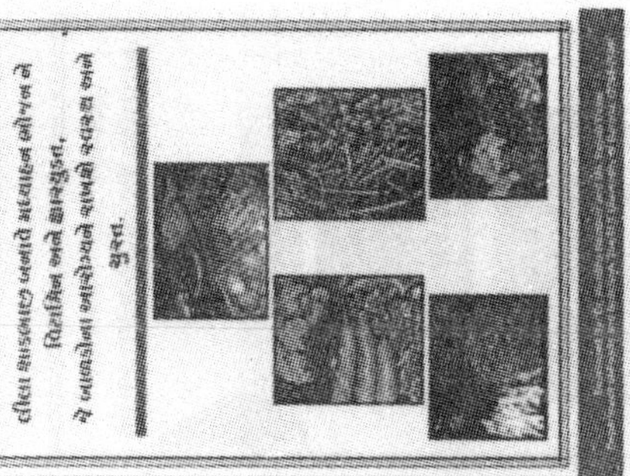

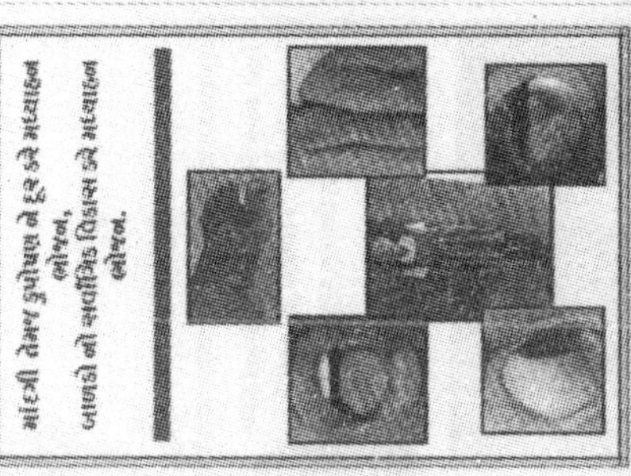

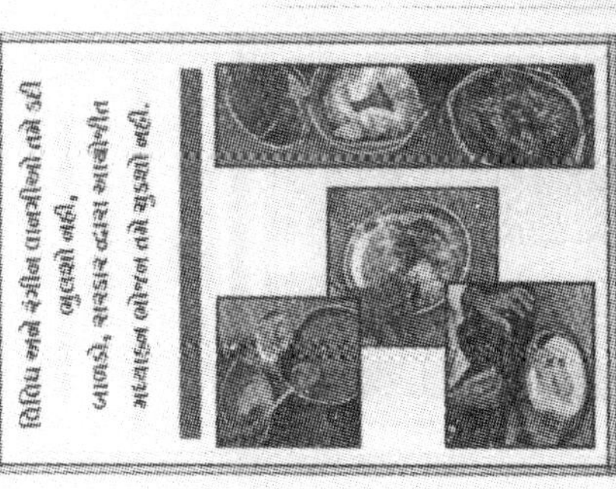

Poster 5 to 8

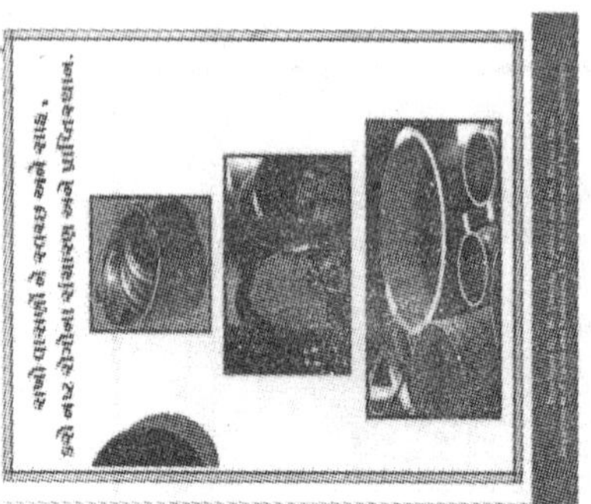

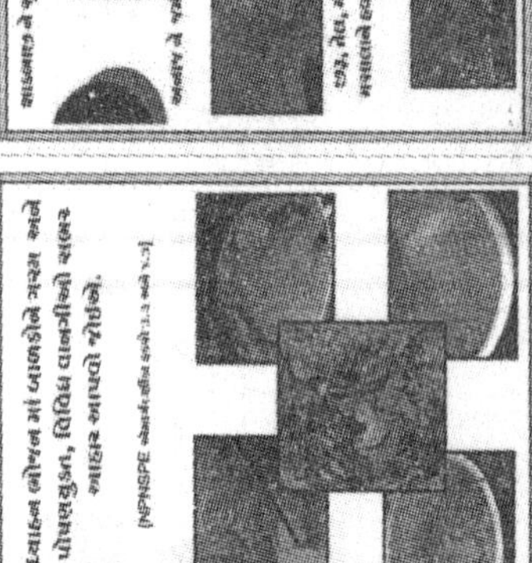

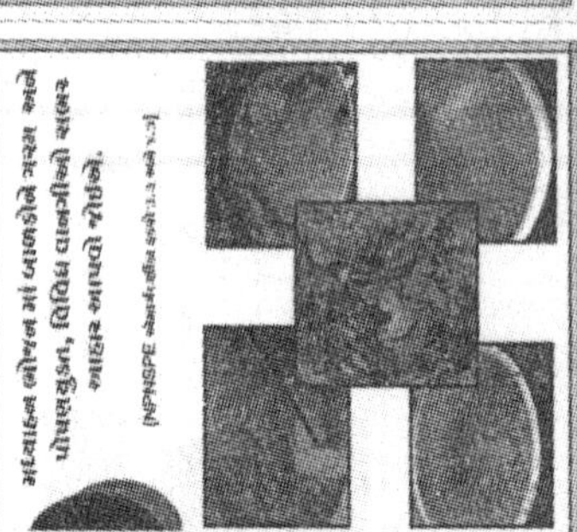

Poster 9 and 10

નવો મધ્યાહન ભોજન

દિવસ અને મેનુ		પિરસવા ની યોગ્ય માત્રા	ઊર્જા (કેલેરી)	પ્રોટીન (ગ્રામ)
સોમવાર	સાંભાર-ભાત અને શિરો ([illegible])		૬૭૫	૧૭
મંગળવાર	દાળ-પાલક અને ભાત ([illegible])		૫૦૯	૧૨
બુધવાર	વઘારેલી ફાડા ખિચડી અને વઘારેલી છાશ ([illegible])		૪૮૮	૧૬
ગુરુવાર	લાપસી અને દૂધી-દાળ શાક ([illegible])		૫૬૯	૧૨
શુક્રવાર	વેજિટેબલ પુલાવ ભાત ([illegible])		૫૦૬	૧૨
શનિવાર	વઘારેલી ખિચડી અને મિક્સ શાક ([illegible])		૫૨૨	૧૨

શાકભાજી નો વપરાશ

૧. રોજના મા ઓછામાં ઓછી ૧૨ કિલો, અને વિવિધ પ્રકારની શાકભાજી રોજે વાપરવી.
૨. ટામેટા, બટાકા, પાલક, સરગવાની શિંગ, વટાણા, પાપડી, કોથમિર, દૂધી, ફુલાવર, કાકડી, મેથી, વિગેરે જેવી શાકભાજીઓ વાપરવી.
૩. એક દિવસ મા ૫ જુદી જુદી શાકભાજીઓ વાપરવી.

DEVELOPED BY: Dr. VANISHA NAMBIAR & Ms. RUJUTA DESAI
DEPARTMENT OF FOODS AND NUTRITION,
THE M.S.UNIVERSITY OF BARODA, 2008-09

દૈનિક રાશન ના વપરાશ માટેની માર્ગદર્શિકા - કિશોરી માટે

લાભાર્થીઓ ની સંખ્યા	મેનુ પ્રમાણે દિવસ ના રાશન નો વપરાશ (કિલો)																							
	સોમવાર સાંભાર – ભાત અને શિરો				મંગળવાર દાળ - પાલક અને ભાત				બુધવાર વઘારેલી ફાડા ખિચડી અને વઘારેલી છાશ				ગુરુવાર લાપસી અને દૂધી–દાળ - શાક				શુક્રવાર વેજિટેબલ પુલાવ - ભાત				શનિવાર વઘારેલી ખિચડી અને મિક્સ શાક			
	ઘઉં	ચોખા	દાળ	તેલ	ઘઉં	ચોખા	દાળ	તેલ	ઘઉં	ચોખા	દાળ	તેલ	ઘઉં	ચોખા	દાળ	તેલ	ઘઉં	ચોખા	દાળ	તેલ	ઘઉં	ચોખા	દાળ	તેલ
૧૦૦	૫	૫	૨	૧	–	૧૦	૨	૧	૧૦	–	૩	૧	૬	–	૨	૧	–	૧૦	૨	૧	–	૧૦	૪	૧
૧૫૦	૭.૫	૭.૫	૩	૧.૫	–	૧૫	૩	૧.૫	૧૫	–	૪.૫	૧.૫	૯	–	૩	૧.૫	–	૧૫	૩	૧.૫	–	૧૫	૬	૧.૫
૨૦૦	૧૦	૧૦	૪	૨	–	૨૦	૪	૨	૨૦	–	૬	૨	૧૨	–	૪	૨	–	૨૦	૪	૨	–	૨૦	૮	૨
૨૫૦	૧૨.૫	૧૨.૫	૫	૨.૫	–	૨૫	૫	૨.૫	૨૫	–	૭.૫	૨.૫	૧૫	–	૫	૨.૫	–	૨૫	૫	૨.૫	–	૨૫	૧૦	૨.૫
૩૦૦	૧૫	૧૫	૬	૩	–	૩૦	૬	૩	૩૦	–	૯	૩	૧૮	–	૬	૩	–	૩૦	૬	૩	–	૩૦	૧૨	૩
૩૫૦	૧૭.૫	૧૭.૫	૭	૩.૫	–	૩૫	૭	૩.૫	૩૫	–	૧૦.૫	૩.૫	૨૧	–	૭	૩.૫	–	૩૫	૭	૩.૫	–	૩૫	૧૪	૩.૫
૪૦૦	૨૦	૨૦	૮	૪	–	૪૦	૮	૪	૪૦	–	૧૨	૪	૨૪	–	૮	૪	–	૪૦	૮	૪	–	૪૦	૧૬	૪
૪૫૦	૨૨.૫	૨૨.૫	૯	૪.૫	–	૪૫	૯	૪.૫	૪૫	–	૧૩.૫	૪.૫	૨૭	–	૯	૪.૫	–	૪૫	૯	૪.૫	–	૪૫	૧૮	૪.૫
૫૦૦	૨૫	૨૫	૧૦	૫	–	૫૦	૧૦	૫	૫૦	–	૧૫	૫	૩૦	–	૧૦	૫	–	૫૦	૧૦	૫	–	૫૦	૨૦	૫
શાકભાજી	૧૦-૧૨ કિલો શાકભાજી રોજની વાપરવી; દરેક મેનુ મા ૫ સ્વસ્થ લીલા શાકભાજી નો વાપરવી																							

Developed by: Dr. Vanisha Nambiar and Ms. Rujuta Desai, Department of Foods and Nutrition, M.S University of Baroda, Vadodara. 2008-09

Data base from the present study is a novel approach to improve the MDM in India, and can be replicated for improvement in the quality of services delivered by the grass root level workers, which in turn would help in the overall improvement of the MDMP.

CONCLUSION

Use of a Positive Deviance Approach and BCC strategy with the MDM staff, teaching staff as well as the students helped to bring about a change in various positive practices related to quality of MDM namely cleanliness, food handling storage and serving and monitoring by teachers. Thus the following study highlights the fact that use of a *positive deviant approach (PDA)* for improving MDM is a sustainable strategy and can be used extrapolated for improvement of other MDM centres.

7 Recommendations

Thus to conclude, though a huge amount of money has been allotted to MDMP it still lacks the basic infrastructure for its successful implementation. Efforts need to be taken to improve the infrastructure of kitchen, store room and school infrastructure. The MDM staff should be given knowledge regarding the programme and its objectives, they need to be trained regarding hygienic habits and an increase in their salary should be made.

Quality and quantity of the meal should be improved to increase the number of beneficiaries and to improve the nutritional status of the children. Teachers should be made aware of their responsibilities towards the programme and their role in improving the health status of children by educating them about hygienic habits and importance of healthy foods.

Menus need to be modified and staff should be trained to prepare nutritious recipes by incorporating more of vegetables and new methods or recipes of fortified wheat flour should be included. Regular monitoring of the programme should be done by the government officials, Gram panchayat and community people which would help to improve the programme.

The following section highlights these suggestions under specific headings.

INFRASTRUCTURE OF MDM CENTERS AND SCHOOLS

The infrastructure needs to be improved. Many schools didn't have kitchen sheds, separate store rooms, safe food storage facilities and proper water and toilet facilities.

- A separate Kitchen shed and store room should be constructed in schools which should be located at a distance away from classrooms such that it does not disturb the teaching process.
- Store rooms should have shelves/cupboards for safe storage of spices and utensils and an elevated platform should be made to store the raw materials.
- The roof of the kitchen and store room should be intact and the area should be well lighted and ventilated.
- Gas cylinders should be provided for cooking food or smokeless chullhas should be provided which would become easy for the staff to cook food. Fire extinguishers or buckets of sand and water should be kept near the kitchen area as a safety measure.
- Cemented/tiled service area covered with roof should be made which would create a clean and pleasant surrounding for the children consuming MDM.
- A water tank should be constructed near the kitchen and water purifying tablets should be used to make it potable and safe for drinking.
- Toilets should be made functional and sanitation and hygiene aspects should be maintained.
- Food safety laws should be implemented by the government with respect to food hygiene, personal hygiene, environmental hygiene and HACCP approach should be applied in the entire system.
- Adequate utensils should be provided for preparing recipes such as equipments for making Chapattis, Pressure cookers for cooking Dals etc.

GRASSROOT LEVEL WORKERS

- The MDM staff should be educated regarding health and nutrition, personal hygiene and safe food handling practices.
- Education on food safety should be imparted to the food handlers to maintain the food prepared safe and hygienic.
- The staff should be given uniforms or a pair of clothes that should be worn during working in kitchen.
- The salary of the staff needs to be raised in comparison to the quantum of work done.
- The number of staff should be adequate according to the number of students in school.

RECIPES AND MENU

- Variety in the menu should be incorporated to hold the interest of students and increase the number of beneficiaries. The menu should be modified to include vegetables (green leafy vegetables and seasonal vegetables) to improve the nutritional quality of MDM.
- Standardized cups and spoons should be used for serving the Mid Day Meal to the children in schools.
- Weighing balances should be present at the MDM centers for weighing the raw materials supplied to the schools and for allocating ration according to the guidelines per child.
- School kitchen gardens with fruits and vegetables (seasonal) should be developed which can be used in preparing Mid Day Meals.
- Fortified wheat flour recipes should be modified such that their appearance and taste is acceptable to the children.
- Standardized procedures should be laid down for preparing the meals at all centers and training should be given to the staff for following these methods during meal preparation.

ROLE OF TEACHERS IN MDMP

- Teachers should be made aware of their responsibilities in monitoring the programme right from the raw materials received at the centers and usage of ration till preparing of the Mid Day Meal and serving to the children.
- They should impart nutrition and health education and hygienic habits to the children like hygiene practices during eating, cleaning and washing plates before having the food and personal and environmental hygiene.
- Teachers should be playing an active role in the programme and should not consider MDM to be an additional work load.
- Teachers should taste the food for its quality and wholesomeness and monitor while the meal is served to the children.
- They should be aware of the norms of the programme which would help them to effectively monitor the usage of ration and vegetables in the menu to reduce the chances of manipulation of the raw materials and money given for buying of vegetables.
- They should motivate all the children in school to consume Mid Day Meal and make them aware of the nutritional aspects provided to them through the meals.
- They should educate the parents about the objectives and benefits of the programme.

PARTICIPATION OF PARENTS AND COMMUNITIES

- Parents, Sarpanch and organisations should be involved for successful implementation of the programme. School development management committee should be developed which involves the head teacher of the school, parents and elected members of the village government.
- Parents should be educated regarding the importance of health and nutrition among children and strategies to overcome malnutrition.

- Parents should be made aware of the importance of MDM and that it is a supplementary meal and not a substitute of the meal at home.
- Sarpanch, village people and organisations like NGOs should provide free meals "Tithi Bhojan" to the school children atleast once a month and donate plates, utensils etc or money to the schools.
- Parents and community members should supervise the MDM preparation which would maintain the quality and nutritional standards of the meal.
- The government officials should be trained and educated in successful implementation of the programme.

NUTRITION AND HEALTH INTERVENTION

Improving the health and nutritional status of the children is one of the objectives of the programme. The nutritional status of the children was assessed in the present study which indicated a large number of children still falling under malnutrition category.

- Health checkups should be done regularly by the school health programme. Micronutrient supplementation of Iron and Vitamin A and deworming tablets should be given to the children along with the Mid Day Meal to reduce the problem of malnutrition to a great extent.
- The height and weight of the children should be measured regularly as part of school health activity. Severely stunted and thin children should be identified by the teachers and a large part of MDM and priority in health care services should be given to these children. Regular monitoring of the height and weight of these children should be done at every 3 months interval.
- Health awareness activities and workshops should be conducted for educating parents, teachers, MDM staff and children regarding healthy eating, healthy practices and healthy environment by the health department. Posters showing the hygienic habits, healthy diet and personal hygiene should be displayed in class rooms.

References

Afridi F. (2009), Mid-Day Meals in Two States: Comparing the Financial and Institutional Organisation of the Programme, Economic and Political Weekly.

Alexandre R, Marra M D, Luciana R N and Carla M P. (2010), Positive Deviance: A New Strategy for Improving Hand Hygiene Compliance, Infection Control and Hospital Epidemiology, 31:1.

Alur A, Nath S and Kumar P. (2005), Participatory Monitoring and Evaluation-Field Experience, NGO Programme Karnatak – Tamil Nadu Series 1.

Anding J D, Boleman C and Thompson B. (2006), Self-reported Changes in Food Safety Behaviours Among Food Service Employees: Impact of a Retail Food Safety Education Programme, Journal of Food Science education: Vol. 6, No. 4. 72-76.

Aspatwar AP and Bapat MM (1995), Vitamin A Status of Socio-economically Backward Children.

AWP and Budget. (2008-09) (Annual Work Plan and Budget) National Programme of Nutritional Support to Primary Eduction, Government of Madhya Pradeshy.

Bakshi M and Sharma D. (2008), Strategies for Control of Anaemia in School Age Population. Unpublished Dissertation Thesis, Department of Foods and Nutrition. Faculty of Home Science, Maharaja Sayajirao University of Baroda, Baroda, Gujarat.

Bergeron G. (1999), Rapid Appraisal Methods for the Assessment, Design, and Evaluation of Food Security Programmes, International Food Policy Research Institute 2033 K Street, N.W. Washington, D.C. 20006 U.S.A.

Biggs S. (2005), Learning from the Positive to Reduce Rural Poverty: Institutional Innovations in Agricultural and Natural Resources Research and Development, School of Development Studies, University of East Anglia, Norwich, NR4 7TJ, U.K.

Brick W. (2009), Macrocytosis.

CART (Center for Consumer Action). (2007), Pilot Study 5 Rajasthan, India: An Assessment of the Mid-Day Meal Scheme.

Census (2001), (Provisional). Literates and Literacy Rates.

Census (2011), Census Report India.

Census of India (2001).

Charavarty K. (2010), India, Karnataka: No Toilets in Half of State's Schools. Deccan Herald.

Chugh S. (2008), A Study of Best Practices in the Implementation of Mid-Day Meal Programme in Maharashtra. Department of Comparative Education and International Cooperation, National University of Educational Planning and Administration.

Corlien M.V., Pathmanathan I and Brownlee A. (2003), Designing and Conducting Health Systems Research Projects, Volume I: Proposal Development and Fieldwork, International Development Research Centre in Association with WHO Regional Office for Africa, KIT Publishers, Amsterdam.

DDWS (2010-11), Department of Drinking Water Supply, Ministry of Rural Development, Demand No.83.

De A, Noronha C and Samson M. (2005), Towards more Benefits from Delhi's Midday Meal Scheme, Collaborative Research and Dissemination (CORD), New Delhi, October.

De J R. (2008), Strategies to Cope Up With Disparities in Health Services in India. June 4.

Department of School Education and Literacy (2007), An Environmental Assessment, Ministry of Human Resources Development Government of India, New Delhi.

Dreze J and Goyal A. (2003), Future of Mid Day Meals. Economic and Political Weekly. 1, November.

DWCRA (Development of Women And Children In Rural Areas).

EAS (Employment Assurance Scheme).

Elizabeth HB, Leslie AC, Shoba R, Laura R, Ingrid MN and Harlan MK. (2009), Research in Action: Using Positive Deviance to Improve Quality of Health Care, Implementation Science.

FAO (Food Agriculture Organaization) (2004), School Garden Concept Note, Improving Child Nutrition and Education Through Promotion of School Garden Programme, Food and Agriculture Organisation of the United Nations (FAO); Rome.

Ghuman B.S and Akshat (2009), Mehta Health Care Services in India: Problems and Prospects.

Global Hunger Index Report (2008), The Challenge of Hunger 2008: Global Hunger Index.

Godkar BP (1998), Book of Medical Research Technology.

Gragnolati M, Shekar M, Gupta M D, Bredenkamp C and Lee Y K (2005), India's Undernourished Children: A Call for Reform and Action.

Gupta PK (1989), Health Status of Rural School Children. Indian Pediatr., 26(6):581-4.

Gupta R, Rastogi P and Arora S (2003), Low Obesity and High Undernutrition Prevalence in Lower Socio-economic Status School Girls: A Double Jeopardy.

Hematocrit or Packed Cell Volume.

Hopkins WG. (2000), Quantitative Research Design.

Part-III Plan Outlay (2010-2011), Expenditure Budget Vol. I.

Huebler F. (2007), India has 21 Million Children Out of School.

Huff M. (2000), Anemia.

ICDS (Integrated Child Development Services) Scheme.

IFPRI (International Food Policy Research Institute). (2008), Global Hunger Index- a Basis for Cross Country Comparisons.

INSA (Indian National Science Academy). (2009), Nutrition Security for India– Issues and way forward, A Position paper.

IRDP. Self-Employment Programmes-Integrated Rural Development Programme.

Iyer U. and Dhaundiyal G. (2010), Impact of Mid Day Meal Programme on the Growth and Hemaoglobin Status of School Going Children: A Comparative Study Between NGO (The Akshay Patra Foundation) and Non-NGO Intervention.

Iyer U. and Roy S. (2007), An Exploratory Study on the Nutritional Status of Urban and Rural Adolesecent Children (12-16 Years) of Vadodara District. M.Sc Dissertation Thesis. Foods and Nutrition Department, M.S. University of Baroda, Baroda, Gujarat, India.

Iyer U. and Shah S. (2005), Assessment of Nutritional Status of Adolescent Children (10-18 Years) in an Urban School of Vadodara. M.Sc Dissertation Thesis. Foods and Nutrition Department, M.S. University of Baroda, Baroda, Gujarat, India.

Kanani S. and Elayath N. (2008), Programme Evaluation of the Urban Mid-Day Meal In Vadodara City and Assessing its Contribution to the Nutritional Status and Educational Achievements of the School Child. Unpublished Dissertation Thesis. Department of Foods and Nutrition. Faculty of Home Science, Maharaja Sayajirao University of Baroda, Baroda, Gujarat.

Kanani S. (1994), Feeding the Hungry School Child: Process Evaluation of the MDMP in Baroda City. Department of Foods and Nutrition. Faculty of Home Science, Maharaja Sayajirao University of Baroda, Gujarat.

Kanani S. (1984), Intervention Studies with Antiparasitics, Vitamin A and Iron Supplementation on Mid Day Meal Programme Beneficiaries. Doctoral Thesis, Department of Foods and Nutrition, M S University of Baroda, Baroda, India.

Kannaiyan S. (2006), Report on Right to Food Campaign, Tamil Nadu. Economical and Political Weekly.

Kapil U and Sethi V. (2004), Prevalence of Undernutrition Amongst Children (6-9 Years) in Delhi, Indian J Peadiatr; 41, 628-629.

Kaushal S. (2009), A Study of Best Practices in the Implementation of Mid-Day-Meal Programme in Rajasthan. National University of Educational Planning and Administration.

Khera R. (2006), Mid-Day Meals in Primary Schools: Achievements and Challenges. Economic and Political Weekly.

Kotecha P.V., Nirupam S. & Karkar P.D. (2001), Adolescent Girls' Anaemia Control Programme, Gujarat, India, Indian J Med Res 130, pp. 584-589.

Kumar K. (1989), Conducting Key Informant Interviews in Developing Countries. A.I.D. Programme Design and Evaluation Methodology Report no. 13 Agency for International Development.

Kumar R. (2011), Who will Answer the "Future of the Nation," SME World.

Kumar S,P. (2004), Malnutrition.

Kuruvilla A. and Shah B. (2007), Nutrition Health Profile and Impact Evaluation of Nutrition Communication Programme on Knowledge and Perception of Underpriveledged Adolescents (10-19 years) in Urban Slums of Vadodara city. M.Sc Dissertation Thesis. Foods and Nutrition Department, M.S. University of Baroda, Baroda, Gujarat, India.

Labour and Employment Department, Government of Gujarat (2010), Minimum Wages in Gujarat.

Laxmaiah A., Rameshwar Sarma K. V., Hanumantdha Rao D., Gal Reddy Ch., Ravindranath M, Vishnuvardhan Rao M and Vijayaraghavan K. (1999), Impact of Mid Day Meal Programme on Educational and Nutritional Status of School Children in Karnataka. Indian Pediatr 1999; 36: 1221-1228.

Levinson J., Bassetl B. L. and Schultink W. (2004), Utilization of Positive Deviance Analysis in Evaluating Community Based Nutrition Programmes: An Application to the Dular Programme in Bihar, India.

MDG (Milleniuum Development Goal). (2008), The Millennium Development Goals Report, United Nations, New York.

MDG (Milleniuum Development Goal). (2005), The Millennium Development Goals Report, United Nations, United Nations, New York.

MHFW (Ministry of Health and Family Welfare) Annual Report. (2006-2007).

MHRD (Ministry of Human Resource Development). (1997), Department of Education. Government of India.

Ministry of Finance, Annual Budget 2008-09 (2008), Union Budget and Economic Survey; Government of India.

Ministry of Finance, Annual Budget 2008-09. (2008), Union Budget and Economic Survey; Government of India.

Mukhopadhyay A, Bhadra M and Bose K. (2005), Anthropometric Assessment of Nutritional Status of Adolescents of Kolkata, West Bengal, Department of Anthropology, Vidyasagar University, Midnapore 721 102, West Bengal, India.

MWCD (Ministry of Women and Child Development). (2007), Annual Report.

NAC (National Advisory Council). (2004), Mid Day Meal National Advisory Council. Department of School Education and Literacy, Ministry of Human Resource Development, Government of India.

Nambiar V. and Desai R. (2008), A Case Study Report on Evaluation of MDM in 7 Urban Vadodara. A Report Submitted to the Commissioner, Gujarat MDM.

Nambiar V. and Desai R. (2009), An Action Research on Integration of Various Sectors Influencing the Mid Day Meal Programme in Urban Vadodara for its Holistic Upgradation. M.Sc. Dissertation Thesis. Foods and Nutrition Department. M. S. University of Baroda, Vadodara. Gujarat. India.

Nambiar V. and Gandhi N. (2008), Action Project of Augmentation of Vegetables in the Mid Day Meal Scheme of Urban Vadodara and its Evaluation Using Case Study Methodology. Unpublished Dissertation Thesis, Department of Foods and Nutrition, M.S University of Baroda, Baroda, India.

Nambiar V. and Parnami S. (2005), Effect of Drumstick Leaves Supplementation on Hematological Indices of Young Anemic Girls (16-21 yrs). M.Sc Dissertation Thesis. Foods and Nutrition Department, M.S. University of Baroda, Baroda, Gujarat, India.

Nambiar V. and Patel N. (2010), Monitoring and Evaluation of Mid-day Meal Programme in Schools of Rural Vadodara and its Impact on the Nutritional Status of Children (11-16 years).M.Sc Dissertation Thesis. Foods and Nutrition Department, M.S. University of Baroda, Baroda, Gujarat, India.

Nambiar V. and Roy K. (2010), Monitoring and Evaluation of the Mid Day Meal Programme in Tribal Schools of Chhota Udepur and the Impact of the Mid Day Meal Programme on Nutritional Status of Adolescents. M. Sc. Dissertation Thesis. Foods and Nutrition Department, M.S. University of Baroda, Baroda, Gujarat. India.

NFHS 3 (2005-06), Gujarat state report.

NFHS 3 (2005-06), National Family Health Survey 3.

NFI (Nutrition Foundation of India) (2003), A Report of the Workshop on Mid-Day Meal Programmes in Schools in India – The Way Forward. New Delhi.

NP-NSPE (National Programme for Nutritional Support to Primary Education). (2006), Guidelines for Central Assistance Under the National Programme for Nutritional Support to Primary. Department of School Education and Literacy; Government of India.

NRHM (National Rural Health Mission). (2007), Government of India.

PO & RM (Programme Outcome and Response Monitoring). (2005), Summary Record of the First Meeting of the Core Group Constituted for the Programme Outcome and Response Monitoring (PO & RM) Division held Under the Chairmanship of Hon'ble Deputy Chairman (DCH), Planning Commission.

Ramachandran P. (2005), The Double Burden of Malnutrition in India.

Rana K., Santra S., Banerjee T., Mukherjee A. and Kundu M. (2005), Cooked Mid-day Meal Programme in West Bengal – A Study in Birbhum District Pratichi (India) Trust.

Rao N.P. (2004), Evaluation of the Nutrition Programmes. National Institute of Nutrition Hyderabad.

Rath A.K. (2008), Girls Education in India: Achievements Since Independence — Press Release.

Robinson N. (2007), Visiting Madhya Pradesh: A Report on the Implementation of the Mid-Day Meal Scheme in Four Districts of Madhya Pradesh, Yale Fox Fellow at Jawaharlal Nehru University (in association with Vikas Samvad††, Bhopal).

School Sanitation and Hygiene Education. (2004), School Sanitation and Hygiene Education in India, Investment in Building Children's Future, SSHE Global Symposium "Construction is Not Enough" Delft, The Netherlands.

Schuftan C. (1993), Positive Deviance in Child Nutrition: A Critique. Ecol. of Food and Nutrition, Vol. 30, No. 2.

Seidman W. & McCauley M. (2003), The Experts'"Secret Sauce" To Close the Performance Gap, Performance Improvement Journal, Vol. 42; (1); pp. 32-39.

Seshadri S. and Tiwari K. (2000), A Study on Anaemia Control Among Adolescent Girls. Development of a School based Intervention Programme in Kathmandu, Nepal.

Sethi B. (2008), Mid-day Meal Programme and its Impact in Improving Enrollment: A Study in Respect of Rayagada District of Orissa.

Sharma S, Jain Passi S, Thomas S, Gopalan S.H. (2006), Evaluation of Mid Day Meal Programme in MCD Schools. Study Supported by Municipal Corporation of Delhi, Nutrition Foundation of India, Scientific Report.

Sternin M., Sternin J. and Marsh D. (1998), Designing a Community Based Nutrition Programme Using the Hearth Model and the Positive Deviance Approach – A Field Guide.

Steven H.A., Giulio D.I. and Albert M. (2007), Positive and Negative Deviant Workplace Behaviours: Causes, Impacts, and Solutions, Corporate Governance, 1472-0701: Vol. 7, Issue 5: 586-598.

Stewart D.W. and Kamins M.A. (1993), Secondary Research, Information Sources and Methods, Second Edition.

Swaminathn P., Jeyaranjan J., Sreenivasan R. and Jayashree K. (2004), Tamil Nadu's Midday Meal Scheme – Where Assumed Benefits Score Over Hard Data. Economic and Political Weekly.

Tholakele and Mpumalanga. (2003), The Integrted Nutrition Programme, Kwa-Zulu Natal.

UNICEF (2010).

Vossenaar M., Mayorga E., Marý´a Jose´ Soto-Me´ndez. (2009), The Positive Deviance Approach Can Be Used to Create Culturally Appropriate Eating Guides Compatible with Reduced Cancer Risk1–3. J. Nutr. 139: 755-762.

World Bank Report. (2009), World Bank Report on Malnutrition in India.

Index